Finally Free!

Finally Free!

The Easy Way to STOP SMOKING for Women

ALLEN CARR

ARCTURUS

With special thanks to the amazing women in our international team of therapists for their invaluable help with this book and also to Ian McLellan, Charles Cooper, Niko Heyng, Nigel Matheson, Tim Glynne-Jones, Sophie Bowley-Aicken and the rest of the team at Arcturus Publishing. Thank you for playing your part in curing millions of smokers worldwide.

ARCTURUS

This edition published in 2013 by Arcturus Publishing Limited
26/27 Bickels Yard, 151–153 Bermondsey Street,
London SE1 3HA

ISBN: 978-1-84858-979-7
AD002473EN

Printed in China

INTRODUCTION

I stopped smoking in August 1988, and I have never stopped being grateful to Allen Carr. Without him, not only would I not be here writing these words, but, most probably, I would not be here at all. THANK YOU, ALLEN! In 2003, I was entrusted with translating and publishing *The Easy Way to Stop Smoking* in Italy, where, as in so many other countries, it has remained a bestseller for many years.

Helping Allen to apply the Venus touch in channelling his method specifically for women has been one of the most exciting, enjoyable, and liberating processes of my life. Although Allen Carr's original book works just as well for women as it does for men, women perceive many of the issues associated with smoking differently. There are particular difficulties faced by women who want to quit, including those arising from perceived links between cigarettes and fashion, style, sex, glamour, stress relief and weight control. In *Finally Free!*, every aspect of smoking is examined from a female perspective, providing answers to female-specific questions and concerns.

It is natural for you to be nervous and sceptical at this point – I remember having those feelings myself before I stopped smoking – but read on with an open mind. We have nothing but good news for you!

Francesca Cesati,
Allen Carr's Easyway, International Therapist Team

CHAPTER 1

Question everything you've been told

Women have achieved something remarkable in the last one hundred years. The role of women in society has been revolutionized, from a position of subservience to a position of power, in business, politics and the church.

A damaging situation that had no basis in logic has been checked, challenged and changed.

Ask yourself how that revolution for women was brought about. Look at its pioneers: courageous women who dared to challenge popular perceptions and rules.

Had all women had the same mentality as those brave pioneers, it would surely not have taken a hundred years to reach the situation we are in today.

But for every pioneer who refuses to accept the status quo, there are many more who:

- agree with the principles but are afraid to act.
- bury their heads in the sand and accept the way things are.

It's the same across both sexes.

And it's the same with smoking.

BRAINWASHING

To effect a radical change in the ideas and beliefs of a person.

Brainwashing applies to practically every aspect of our lives. We are concerned with just two aspects: brainwashing as it relates to smoking and brainwashing as it relates to the differences between men and women.

We all know that smoking is filthy and disgusting and it ruins our health and wealth.

Everyone who picks up this book wants to achieve the same thing: to put out the final cigarette and never want to smoke another.

So why haven't you done it?

'I don't know how I'd get by without cigarettes.'

You will know of many ex-smokers who have managed to quit through sheer willpower. For weeks, months, even years you watched them struggling, trying all the pills, patches and gum to give them a bit of relief. And even now, when you're out together enjoying a drink and a catch-up, you can see the yearning in their eyes when you light up.

The difference between smokers and non-smokers

It's not just that one smokes and the other doesn't. It's that a non-smoker has never experienced the desire to smoke. Before you lit your first cigarette, you never felt that desire either.

Don't you want to be like a non-smoker – like you were before you ever lit your first cigarette? Don't you want to live without ever suffering the craving for a cigarette again?

So what is it that keeps pulling you back? Perhaps you think you enjoy it. But who really enjoys:

- sucking toxic fumes into their lungs?
- walking around with the smell of stale smoke on their skin and clothes?
- seeing those little lines appear around the mouth?
- having yellow fingers and brown teeth?
- feeling the repulsion in people they love when they go to kiss them?

Most 20-a-day smokers admit that they only enjoy about two of these cigarettes

You *guess* you enjoy it? You **KNOW** you don't.

Ever wondered why you light up:

- whenever the phone rings?
- whenever you finish a meal?
- whenever you're out with friends?
- whenever you need to concentrate?

Perhaps you think it's just a habit. If it was, you could change it very quickly and easily by locking your cigarettes in a drawer or giving them to someone else to look after. You'd be down from 20 a day to two a day in no time!

But you know that when the urge comes, you would smash open that drawer or fight your best friend to get those cigarettes back.

I've even heard of new mothers who have left their babies in the maternity ward to go in search of cigarettes. The maternal bond is a fearsomely powerful force. Can you think of any other habit for which a mother would break that bond?

'I never feel relaxed if I don't have a cigarette in my hand.'

It is not habit that makes you smoke 20 a day rather than two. Neither is it pleasure. It is a force so powerful that it can threaten even the maternal bond.

It is **FEAR**.

That mother puts her baby at risk because she panics without cigarettes. Why? Because she has been brainwashed into believing that she needs a cigarette to make her feel calm and relaxed.

'I was utterly unconvinced the book would have any effect on me and yet it did. After reading the book properly, something clicked and I've never looked back. It's been six months now and all I feel is happiness that I'm free.'
Rhona M, Scotland

How do we know she's been brainwashed? Because the thing she thinks will cure her pain is the very thing that caused it in the first place.

It's a vicious circle in which pleasure plays no part. And we have a word for that:

ADDICTION

People who have never smoked can't understand the lengths a smoker will go to for the next cigarette. They have never felt that panic caused by withdrawal from nicotine.

They never feel that desire for a cigarette.

This is the real difference between a smoker and a non-smoker. Until you realize this, you will find it very difficult to quit. You will try to become a non-smoker by never smoking again.

That's like placing a bucket in the middle of the kitchen under a leaky roof, rather than repairing the roof. Instead of solving the problem, you merely give yourself another one.

One of the many common misconceptions about all drug addiction is that addicts only suffer withdrawal symptoms when they try to stop using the drug. In truth, they suffer them from the moment the first dose begins to leave their bodies, and the only reason they take the next dose is to try to end the empty, insecure feeling that the previous dose creates.

Until you stop the leak by repairing the hole, your problem will not go away. Until you tackle the cause, your solutions will always be unsatisfactory.

The cause of your smoking problem is your apparent need or desire to smoke.

Non-smokers never have that feeling of need or desire. Just accept this indisputable fact: nobody but yourself forces you to light up.

You might find this difficult to believe, but stopping smoking *is* easy for any smoker, including you. All you need to do is remove the need or desire to smoke.

The need or desire to smoke is the result of brainwashing. Before we ever try a cigarette, we are told that smoking relaxes us, aids concentration and helps to alleviate stress and boredom. We are also told that it is a filthy, disgusting habit that will get us hooked and ruin our health and wealth.

Just accept this indisputable fact: nobody but yourself forces you to light up

Ironically, the people who most emphasize the downside are often puffing away as they do so.

There is not a smoker in the entire history of the planet who believed they would become hooked when they took their first drag.

It is only after we fall into the trap that the brainwashing takes effect. We no longer see smoking as filthy and disgusting but as something enjoyable, relaxing and a real confidence booster. Soon we are regarding cigarettes as indispensable and it's not long before we are unable to go without them.

No matter how quickly or gradually this process occurs, we seem oblivious to it. But there is no denying that our perceptions have shifted. The question is, which is the correct perception?

CHAPTER 2

Separating fact from fiction

When asked 'How did Allen Carr help you to stop?' some ex-smokers who have attended my clinics will reply, to my horror, 'He brainwashed me into believing that I didn't need ever to smoke again.'

This implies that it will be a simple matter for someone to reverse the process and convince these smokers that they do need to smoke again.

Let me emphasize: I never use brainwashing techniques. In fact, my method – which I call Easyway – is based on counter-brainwashing.

I define counter-brainwashing as: 'A technique designed to remove the brainwashing to enable the person **to see the true situation**.'

When I refer to 'smoking', as I do throughout the book, take this to mean any form of taking nicotine, including tobacco, snuff, chewing gum, patches or nasal sprays.

That doesn't mean I'm going to bombard you with horrific statistics about what smoking costs you in terms of both wealth and health. I would if I thought it would achieve my goal of freeing you from the nicotine trap, but actually it would be counter-productive.

You are already aware that smoking is bad for your health and this knowledge creates anxiety. What do smokers do when they feel anxious? They reach for a cigarette.

Fear of success

The main factor preventing smokers from even attempting to stop is fear. This fear is real and takes many forms. Ironically, the greatest fear is the fear of success: the fear that life will not be enjoyable without cigarettes. After all, we've seen our friends suffer when they've tried to give up. Who wants to be like that?

Society tends to treat smokers as rather simple-minded, weak-willed pariahs. The majority of smokers see themselves in a similar light.

This too is all part of the brainwashing. In fact, you have as much willpower – possibly more – than the next person, be they non-smoker or ex-smoker. Right now, it's what keeps you smoking in the face of the knowledge that it's killing you.

You might find some of the things I say in this book difficult to believe. At times you might be tempted to hurl it in the bin. Please don't do that. There are no horror stories in these pages.

'Fear? Losing my ciggies, that's what I call fear!'

On the contrary, **I have nothing but good news for you.**

'Attended an Allen Carr session and haven't looked back. Feel absolutely fantastic and continue to be a very happy non-smoker.'
Debbie B, Bristol

Which comes first, the addiction or the fear?

The truth of the matter is that the addiction creates the fear and the fear strengthens the addiction. Whichever way smokers look at their problem, fear prevents them from doing anything about it.

One ingenuity of the nicotine trap is that, like all drug addiction, it is designed to keep you hooked. The more it harms your health and purse, the more you cling to it.

The tug-of-war of fear

Smokers see smoking as a sort of tug-of-war. On one side, there's fear of the harm it's doing them. On the other side, there's the fear of coping without it.

The first fear is a projection into the future. The second becomes immediate the moment you make an attempt to stop. Naturally the tendency is to opt for the fear that might never happen.

'You free me from the evil weed?!! I'd like to see that.'

The beautiful truth is that all your fears can be removed before you finish the book. As we undo the brainwashing that has kept you hooked, you will realize that your fears are founded on a myth. So I want you to make a promise that you will complete the book.

But why should you trust me? Why should you put your faith in a book, just because it claims to offer an easy escape from the nicotine trap? It's a fair question. Now I have one for you.

What will happen if you don't?

We all accept that life is a gamble. But how many times in our lives are we in the position of having absolutely nothing to lose and everything to gain from a decision we make?

You are in that enviable position now. Be aware that the trap is designed to imprison you for life. Don't allow yourself to be fooled by it. If you complete the book

Don't delay
The damage caused by smoking is cumulative. But no matter how old you are, stopping smoking will have immediate benefits for your health. You will immediately begin to feel better.

YOU HAVE ABSOLUTELY NOTHING TO LOSE!

It's time to get happy. Focus on the incredible gains you stand to make. There is far more to gain from Easyway than simply keeping more cash in your purse or smelling sweeter.

'Thank you for giving me my life. My life began when I stopped smoking'

We receive comments like this all the time. They come in letters and emails from people who have quit thanks to Easyway: female and male; heavy, long-term smokers and younger people who feared a lifetime of slavery.

Waiting for a miracle

The ingenuity of the trap makes us put off any attempt to quit in the hope that we will just wake up one day and find we no longer have the desire or the need to smoke cigarettes. There is a small minority of smokers for whom such dreams do come true. Sadly, for most of us that day never comes or comes too late. Please don't let that happen to you.

When the fog is lifted from your eyes, it is like waking from a nightmare. That feeling is waiting for you. That's why I want you to promise to finish this book. I want you to enjoy that wonderful feeling of being a non-smoker.

Most smokers start smoking in their youth and, as the years pass, associate a loss of joie de vivre with growing older. When you become a non-smoker again, you realize that the joy is still there – you just couldn't see it because of the trap.

It is like a bonus. When you first decide to quit, you look forward to feeling healthier and wealthier. You can't imagine the other benefits that will come your way.

• **Self-loathing replaced with self-respect**
The inability to control the addiction makes us despise ourselves, often more than we realize. When you quit, the sense of achievement is a huge boost to your self-esteem.

• **Insecurity replaced with unconditional confidence**
Once you realize that you can cope with stress, concentration or social situations without a cigarette, and indeed handle them better and enjoy them more, it does wonders for your confidence.

• **Removal of that black shadow**
The ever-increasing feeling of misery and fear at the back of our minds that gets worse and worse the deeper we sink into the nicotine trap.

• Ending the slavery

Smoking is a chore that causes endless torment. When you aren't allowed to do it, you wish you could, and when you are allowed to, you wish you didn't have to.

The sum total of the benefits of stopping smoking is greater than any of the individual gains. The statement, 'My life began when I stopped smoking', says it all.

One of the most inspiring letters we ever received was from a young lady called Debbie Sekula. She began:

'I laughed to myself about how I had become so desperate to stop smoking that I was resorting to a book. It seemed illogical and pathetic. It made no sense that scientifically devised methods of quitting smoking would fail and a book would succeed.'

In the world of the nicotine addict, though, everything you think you know about the trap and how you are supposed to get out of it is usually the complete opposite of the truth.

This book will change the way you perceive cigarettes for the rest of your life. Knowledge is power: without it you feel at a loss; with it you feel like a winner.

Debbie continued:

'It was then that I was overcome with the knowledge that I had a smile on my face that I could not get rid of. As I

turned the final page of your book that Sunday afternoon, I knew that I would never smoke again! I knew that, once and for all, I was cured.

'I am experiencing a new world of smells, taste, energy. I can't believe how great I feel! My life at the moment is one big miracle. You opened the door for me to walk through and I can't thank you enough.

'You talk about a revelation that can happen any time over three weeks or so. With me it was seconds! I don't even think about smoking any more.'

The language we non-smokers use about that moment of revelation is quite dramatic.

The words 'miracle' and 'magic' recur with unorring froquoncy. But there is no magic in Easyway.

It may seem like a miracle, but this is not hocus pocus.

This is fact.

New lease of life

Many smokers think life won't be worth living without cigarettes. In fact, it's not long before smokers who stop find a new lease of life. They tend to take more exercise, they eat much more healthily and their social life gets better because their self-image is more positive. The truth is, there are no drawbacks to stopping smoking as long as you find it easy to do so.

One step at a time

Continue to smoke while you read this book.

That might sound like odd advice, but I've seen how distracted smokers get when they try to quit before they're ready. I want your full attention while you're reading and I assure you that by the end you will be ready to stop.

Don't use this as an excuse to read one line a day!

If you've not smoked for a day or so, then just carry on reading without smoking, confirming at the end of the book that you have already smoked your final cigarette.

CHAPTER 3

Neither miracle nor magic

Many years after becoming a non-smoker, it still feels like a miracle took place. What was different about this method from all the others that had failed me? Sometimes I would stop for months on end but I never felt like a non-smoker.

I never felt the joy that I felt when I quit for good using my Easyway method. I even believed – no doubt as you currently believe – that there were different types of smoker.

SOCIAL SMOKERS
These people just seem to be going through the motions. They always look uncomfortable, never inhale, keep forgetting to flick the ash and, as a rule, never buy their own.

CASUAL SMOKERS
These are the type that every 'heavy' smoker envies. They appear to enjoy each cigarette immensely, yet they only ever seemed to need or desire about five cigarettes a day.

HABITUAL SMOKERS
These smoke around 20 a day but only apparently enjoy two of them. They seem to have drifted into the habit and claim they would stop if it began to affect their health.

REAL SMOKERS
Deep down inside, they feel as if they are completely dependent on tobacco and, as a result of years of brainwashing, they are also convinced they couldn't possibly enjoy life, concentrate or handle stress without a cigarette.

To go from the misery of being a 'real smoker' to the joy of being a non-smoker does feel like a miracle. It is as if someone has lifted a thick and ever-present veil from your eyes: suddenly you can see smoking without the brainwashing.

To go from the misery of being a 'real smoker' to the joy of being a non-smoker does feel like a miracle

It isn't a miracle. It is a simple scientific method that cannot fail if you follow it closely.

'Your book has changed my thinking about smoking. I do not feel like I am missing out on anything in quitting this time.'
Trish, Michigan

How can you make it happen to you? Easily. And the good news is you've already started. All you have to do is complete the book with an open mind.

The next question is why?

- 'Why does this method work where others fail?'
- 'Why is it so easy?'
- 'Why doesn't everyone use it if it's that good?'

These questions will remain in your mind through this book. The last one is a question that still baffles me. Just make sure the questions don't deflect you from the simple process of reading through the book and understanding what I say.

Question everything

That was the message in Chapter 1. Question both your brainwashed perception of cigarettes and the facts I tell you, so you can make your own informed choices.

Scare tactics

As long as we still have the brainwashing, no amount of fear for our health will make us quit. In fact, it makes us smoke more, because when smokers feel fear – what do they do? – they smoke. You only have to look outside the main door of any hospital to know this is true.

If there are all these different types of smokers, could it be that you belong to a type that Easyway doesn't work for?

Imagine smoking as a self-imposed prison. It doesn't matter what type of prisoner is in the cell, if they have the key to the door they can all walk out.

Easyway is the key that will enable any smoker to escape immediately from the nicotine trap.

'My friend suggested I try after she had quit. Honestly, I laughed when she raved about your book. But I have not had a craving since I stopped and feel like this is the time that I have really done it. Well, good luck to everyone who quits and BIG THANX to Allen Carr.'

Wendy, New Zealand

I can only give you the key, I cannot force you to use it.

I've probably set you worrying that part of your brain doesn't want you to use that key.

Don't worry about it.

It is normal to have doubts at this stage. Easyway will remove the doubt. Always remember you have absolutely nothing to lose. Finish the book first, then decide if you want to stop. By the end of the book, you'll be free, like Debbie (see page 20).

> Smokers take more time off work than non-smokers. That's often because the act of smoking damages minuscule hair-like structures in the lungs that strain out bacteria, which can cause ailments in the chest and heart. A smoker's cough is the reflex designed to clear partially blocked airwaves and get rid of unwanted materials.

There are several reasons why I've chosen to include Debbie's letter. Let's look again at some of the points she made.

'I laughed to myself about how I had become so desperate to stop smoking that I was resorting to reading a book!'

Debbie was obviously very sceptical about Easyway, as are all smokers in the beginning. Even so, she did finish the book and it's quite obvious that she did succeed. She clearly understood the 'why'.

TrASH theory

The 'experts' at ASH (Action on Smoking and Health) judge success as having gone a year without smoking a cigarette. Why a year? On what scientific evidence is this time-scale based?

If ASH's 'one year' benchmark were valid, no one who had managed to stop for a year would ever get hooked again! Yet there are countless cases of smokers who have stopped for several years and got hooked again.

At our clinics, they are delighted to discover that we remove this need to resist temptation. It might seem like a miracle or magic, but it is based on science, common sense and fact.

Struggling to see the picture?

At this point your view of smoking will be blurred, like one of those 'magic eye' 3D pictures, and while you don't have the correct approach it will remain so. The moment you look at the situation from a re-evaluated standpoint the image will become crystal clear.

Debbie knew she was free before she put out her final cigarette. She didn't have to wait until the second week.

'As I turned the final page of your book that Sunday afternoon, I knew that I would never smoke again! I knew that, once and for all, I was cured.'

You must read this book to the end, to ensure that you are never ever tempted to smoke again

If you enjoy this same experience before you have completed the book, you must still read to the end. It's no good just obtaining the state of euphoria that Debbie so accurately describes; we must ensure that you retain it so that you are never ever tempted to smoke again.

Obnoxious side-effects

Smoking doesn't just harm the smoker. Secondhand smoke not only affects the person who is smoking but everyone around them, including the people they live with.
Secondhand smoke is mostly invisible and odourless, but contains toxic substances such as arsenic and cyanide.

Our proud claim

At our clincs, we have a long-standing policy of refunding a client's fee if they fail to stop smoking for at least three months. More than 80 per cent of clients come to us as a result of word of mouth and, worldwide, fewer than 10 per cent of our clients find it necessary to claim a refund.

The sad fact is that there are smokers who successfully used Easyway for several weeks or even years, only to fall into the trap again.

A so-called 'expert' from the medical profession might knowingly shake his head and say sagely: 'There you see! She wasn't really cured. You can't regard a smoker as cured until they have abstained for at least a year!'

This same 'expert' will conveniently overlook the fact that, as we see time and time again, you cannot regard smokers as cured AFTER they have abstained for a year.

It's not time that measures whether a smoker has successfully managed to become a non-smoker, it's her mental state.

More than 80 per cent of our clients come to us as a direct result of a recommendation

My method is neither magical nor miraculous. Neither is it backed up by powerful institutions like ASH or QUIT, or funded by international drug conglomerates like those pills, patches and other gimmicky substitutes that don't work.

Happy New Year! Not!

To 'give up' smoking is by far the most popular New Year's resolution. I know of several cases where smokers celebrate their first year of abstention by having 'just one' cigarette. Before they know it, they are back in the trap. In such cases it is fair to say that those smokers, far from succeeding because they abstained for a year, failed because they stopped for a year.

I have never advertized, yet my first book, *The Easy Way to Stop Smoking*, has been a bestseller every year since its first publication in 1985. There are now over 150 Easyway clinics in more than 45 countries across every continent with the exception of Antarctica.

If this isn't magic or a miracle, what is it? There is one reason and one reason alone that the method has spread round the globe:

IT WORKS

'Allen Carr? Hah! What does he know?'

CHAPTER 4

How can you ever know when you're cured?

Typically with the 'willpower' method, you start off with a feeling of doom and gloom, yet hopeful that you might succeed if you can survive the misery and craving long enough. But how long is long enough?

We've already established that even 'giving up' for a whole year is not proof against failure.

And so you summon your willpower and you wait. What are you waiting for? Nothing. It's a kind of perpetual torture. You are waiting for nothing to happen.

Willpower in action

When a child has a toy and you take it away, what happens? The child with no willpower will get over the conflict quickly and that will be the end of the matter. But the child with tremendous willpower will go on and on, sometimes into adulthood, dragging up the incident.

Similarly, the complaining ex-smoker will still bemoan the absence of nicotine 20 years after having quit, usually when drunk or confronted by a stressful situation.

Never-ending dilemma
The problem with using a 'willpower' method to stop smoking is that you will always feel you are depriving yourself of a pleasure. Deep in your subconscious, you still believe the brainwashing you have been subjected to all of your life.

The longer you hold out, the longer the torture. You dig deeper and deeper into your reserves but you are only prolonging the agony.

The last time I used the willpower method I survived a full six months without so much as a puff of a cigarette or cigar. After six months I became a nervous wreck, incapable of completing any task that involved even the slightest use of the grey matter. And I gave in.

I despised myself for giving in.

Now that I understand smoking completely (as you are starting to), I realize that no matter how long I had held out, I had no more chance of succeeding than I would have had of skiing up the Matterhorn. I was just using my willpower to prolong the misery.

'I couldn't stop thinking about it, so I started again!'

The life of the person who still feels the need or desire to smoke is miserable whether they carry on or quit

If, when you put out what you hope will be your final cigarette, you still believe that you couldn't enjoy life, or concentrate, or handle stress without smoking, the misery that follows will only reinforce that belief.

Because of the brainwashing, the life of the person who still feels the need or desire to smoke is miserable whether they carry on or quit. It is essential, therefore, to remove the need or desire.

Complete the book, follow my advice and you'll soon know what real pleasure is.

Some people do eventually succeed in quitting using the willpower method. They stick to the task, enduring the hardship, because they have been told it's hard. It never crosses their mind that there might be an easier way. And that is another major flaw with the willpower method: it tells us that we can never be truly free.

Bear in mind that the misery is the result of falling into the trap, not trying to escape from it. Non-smokers never have to suffer such tortures.

Perhaps you have your own idea as to when you'll know you're cured. Give it some serious thought, then compare your answer with the typical answers we receive from clients at our clinics:

When I can go a whole day (week/month) without smoking.

Occasionally you meet long-term smokers who claim to enjoy smoking so much that they've never had the desire to stop. The truth is that they are too frightened to try. Unfortunately, the fact that a smoker hasn't managed to abstain for even a day previously is no guarantee that once they do manage to abstain they'll be free.

When I've gone a year without a cigarette.

This is a very common belief, which we have already addressed. But can you imagine the terror such a statement has on the previous group? No wonder they put off the evil day.

When I can go to a party and enjoy it.

That's more like it, but how do they know they'll enjoy the next party?

When I feel like a non-smoker.

Non-smokers don't feel like non-smokers any more than non-heroin addicts feel like non-heroin addicts or non-carrot eaters feel like non-carrot eaters.

When I can concentrate without a cigarette.

If they believe cigarettes help them to concentrate, whenever they have a mental block they'll sit there craving a cigarette, thereby guaranteeing that they won't be able to concentrate.

I don't know.

Doesn't sound too encouraging, but at least it's honest and it shows they have deduced that the previous answers are inaccurate.

Never!

I used to believe that. I'm so pleased I was wrong.

When I stop thinking about smoking.

I quote Debbie again: *'I don't even think about smoking any more.'*

This is a common theme of the letters we receive, so is it the key to Easyway? After all, one cannot deny that Debbie was happy to be a non-smoker.

'Reading your book, and taking that chance, well, that was the best and most incredible decision I have ever made...'

Yes, Debbie was certainly happy to be a non-smoker, but she'd hardly stopped thinking about smoking. If her letter was anything to go by, she thought about smoking an awful lot, but it didn't make her miserable. It gave her a sense of elation to know that she was no longer enslaved by it.

Not thinking about smoking is a piece of advice from the 'experts' that, more than any other, makes the 'willpower' method such a nightmare.

EXPERT: *'Try to distract your mind. Avoid situations that remind you of smoking.'*

That could mean avoiding home, work and all the places you go to socialize.

EXPERT: *'You're taking this too far. You only need to avoid smokers until you've succeeded.'*

YOU: *'And how long will that be?'*

EXPERT: *'One year. Maybe more.'*

YOU: *'That's helpful! What do you suggest I do in the meantime?'*

It's little wonder that so few smokers manage to succeed when using 'willpower' methods.

So is the key to think happy thoughts whenever you're tempted to light up?

'ISN'T IT GREAT!? I'M FREE! I HAVEN'T THE SLIGHTEST NEED OR DESIRE TO LIGHT UP.'

It might work for a few days, but don't waste your time trying it. It's no good just saying it, you must understand and believe it.

Pink elephants

Don't you find that the more you try NOT to think about something, the more it occupies your mind? Try telling yourself not to think about pink elephants. Now, what's the first thought that comes into your mind?

Mr Carr, how does Easyway work?

Smokers arrive at our clinics in various stages of panic, believing that they have to go through an indefinite period of misery. Most of them leave five or six hours later already happy non-smokers.

What on earth do you say to them?

Do you have five or six hours to spare?

'Happy thoughts? I'd rather have a cigarette!'

I've had this conversation with many inquisitors. They think I'm being evasive. I assure you that I am not. To use Debbie's expression, I open the door for you to walk through. But Debbie didn't experience the euphoria until after she'd walked through that 'door'.

Whether they have the courage to admit it or not, all smokers believe themselves to be stupid, weak-willed people

I'm frequently cornered at social functions by smokers who want to convince me of the pleasure and crutch they get from smoking. I listen patiently, thinking, 'I enjoy eating peas but I don't feel the need to justify it to someone who doesn't.'

When I point out that I can't understand why, if they get so much pleasure from smoking and it is such a crutch for them, they don't encourage their offspring to smoke, they stare at me as if I am the one who is confused.

Most smokers believe themselves to be stupid because they smoke, and a few believe the reverse: that they smoke because they are stupid.

'I was a heavy smoker for 20-plus years. My smokes were more important than anything. I honestly believed that I was doomed to smoke for the rest of my life! Allen Carr's book is a total salvation! Everybody should read it!!!!!'
Kim H, Scotland

Neither statement is true. Even the most intelligent people occasionally do stupid things.

Nobody continues to smoke accidentally, whether they have an incredibly high IQ or not. The vast majority of cigarettes we smoke are smoked subconsciously. However, when we run out, we go out and buy more, or sponge one off another smoker. And that is a deliberate and conscious act.

Get it clearly into your mind: there is a reason for every cigarette that you smoke, and that reason isn't because you are either weak-willed or stupid. You may think you know what the true reason is. If you did, you would have no reason to be reading this book. You would already be a happy non-smoker and would remain one for the rest of your life.

There is a reason for every cigarette that you smoke, and that reason isn't because you are either weak-willed or stupid

The important point is the effect. You started this book feeling down, humble and full of dread, but soon you will feel elated.

Stop worrying about how Easyway works. Debbie started off sceptical but when she finished the book she was euphoric, and even more so over a week later. Millions of smokers have also found it easy to stop smoking by using Easyway.

CHAPTER 5

My claim

Despite whatever promises people may make to you, the truth is that all other methods actually make it more difficult for you to stop.

The current logic of health professionals with regard to smoking is like suggesting to someone who can't swim to try tying their legs together and wearing lead armbands instead of water wings.

If learning to swim meant going through that kind of physical torture, you wouldn't blame anyone for staying out of the pool and taking their chances in life as a non-swimmer, would you?

'Go swimming? Sounds far too dangerous to me, darling. But I will have one of your cigarettes.'

All other methods actually make it more difficult for you to stop

Now imagine that you knew of a method that would enable you to stop smoking

- EASILY, IMMEDIATELY AND PERMANENTLY
- WITHOUT SUFFERING FROM WITHDRAWAL SYMPTOMS
- WITHOUT REQUIRING YOU TO USE WILLPOWER
- WITHOUT REQUIRING YOU TO TAKE PILLS, AIDS OR GIMMICKS OR TO SUFFER AN INITIAL PERIOD OF MISERY
- ALLOWING YOU TO ENJOY SOCIAL OCCASIONS MUCH MORE.

Imagine that you knew of a method that left you

- BETTER EQUIPPED TO HANDLE STRESS
- LESS NERVOUS AND TENSE
- MORE CONFIDENT AND COURAGEOUS
- BETTER ABLE TO CONCENTRATE
- NEVER EVER CRAVING ANOTHER CIGARETTE
- NOT WANTING TO EAT MORE.

What would you say to such a proposition? According to the experts, such a method would be too good to be true. How could it exist? For one thing, it would have the opposite effect of those willpower methods: it would make stopping easy.

Just assume for a moment that such a method did exist and that it had the added bonus of actually allowing you to continue to smoke while you learned how to apply it. Would you need any other method?

I have good news for you. The method I've outlined does exist. I call it Easyway, and you are already starting to use it.

'It's easy to stop smoking. I've done it hundreds of times.'

But if my claim is true, shouldn't the medical profession know about it? And do you not agree that if they recommend any other method they are actually making it harder for their patients to stop?

We have been brainwashed to believe that stopping smoking is incredibly difficult. Yet thousands of smokers have 'given up' overnight without any hassle whatsoever.

You probably know or have heard of people who have quit smoking without any help or any apparent hassle. They don't experience the same feeling of euphoria that Debbie and the majority of ex-smokers who use Easyway describe. Remarkably, though, they find stopping smoking relatively easy. The difference between those smokers and me is that they don't know why they found it so easy.

Before I discovered Easyway, I tried other methods. Some of them actually worked, but only for short periods.

Sometimes at group sessions at our clinics a client will suddenly begin recommending their own 'method' to the other participants. We ask them why they are attending the clinic if their method made it so easy.

'I did something stupid. I had just one cigarette. I didn't even need it…'

We then ask them why they didn't just use their method again?

'I did, but it didn't work this time.'

Society in general, including people who have never smoked, believes it is very difficult to stop smoking. Some smokers even believe it to be impossible. Because this is the received wisdom that we grow up with, it's natural to be sceptical about any method that claims to make it easy.

'My method is great. Shame it hasn't stopped me smoking.'

But imagine you've been learning to swim with your legs tied together and lead armbands on, and then someone tells you about another method that involves untying your legs and wearing water wings. Wouldn't you at least give it a try?

Why should it be difficult to stop, let alone impossible? We've already established that no one but ourselves forces us to light up. So if you decide that you never want to smoke again, why should it be difficult to do just that?

Everyone knows that smoking is a habit and habits are difficult to break.

Both these statements are misleading: we don't smoke out of habit; and even if we did, it would be ridiculously easy to break.

What is a habit?

It's a repeated pattern of behaviour. Get rid of the repetition and there's no habit.

Driven by habit

For most of my life, I've driven on the left-hand side of the road. I don't do this just because I got into the habit of doing it. When I drive in countries where the rule is to drive on the right, I break that habit easily and immediately, for obvious reasons.

'My husband and I both smoked for 8 years. We bought the Easyway book and read it in one day. I haven't touched a cigarette since and it's been three years. I am buying this book for every friend that is a smoker for Christmas.'
Amber, USA

What's of interest is the cause of the repetition.

Habit never explains why we repeat behaviour. To find it easy to break a habit, you need to remove the cause of the habitual behaviour.

In Britain we repeatedly drive on the left because it is a simple law that is easy to understand. Change that law and we find it easy to repeatedly drive on the right.

'It's just a habit, nothing to get concerned about.'

But let us assume that the only reason we continue to smoke is because we have got into the habit of smoking. If that were true, why on earth would the habit be difficult to break? It would be simplicity itself: just don't light another cigarette.

You don't even have to do anything!

I know that the torture is real; I once went through it for six months

The other reason the 'experts' give to explain why 'giving up' is difficult is 'the terrible physical withdrawal symptoms'. This is another myth and just as easy to explode.

Some smokers complain that the withdrawal symptoms feel like flu. If, in order to stop, all we had to do was suffer a bout of flu for a few days, we would jump at the opportunity. The fact is there is no *physical* pain.

Smokers can sleep soundly throughout the night without smoking. They don't wake up pulling their hair out. Many will have tea, coffee or even breakfast first before lighting up their first cigarette of the day. Some will leave the house first and others will wait until they get to work. Even they are not screaming in agony or climbing up the wall.

Where does it hurt?

Next time you feel that 'I want a cigarette' feeling, try describing it. Try pinpointing where it hurts. Can you even remotely fix a point where the sensation occurs? The truth is that you cannot. What you experience is just a growing feeling of unrest and imbalance, which all the time you know you can get rid of by lighting up.

Imagine you reach for your cigarettes and find they're gone. Immediately you will panic and start fumbling around in pockets and drawers, handbags and the like in a frenzied search for nicotine.

That panic feeling smokers get when they are out late at night and supplies are running low starts before the cigarettes run out and gets worse when they are actually smoking the last one. Think about it: at this time, nicotine is going into the body, NOT withdrawing from it. Yet this is the feeling they claim is nicotine withdrawal.

They ration their supply as if it were as precious as water in the desert. But there is no physical pain whatsoever when smokers try to 'give up', and provided they want to stop, the 'habit' is easy to break. This applies not just to you but to all smokers.

Yet it is an undeniable fact that the vast majority of smokers find it exceedingly difficult, if not impossible, to stop.

The reason is fear.

'If you read this book, you will quit smoking. Period. You read the book, quit when you're finished, and that's it. No cravings, no sudden urges to smoke, you don't even miss cigarettes. If you smoke, you literally can't afford not to buy this book.'

CJT, USA

The panic of wanting a cigarette and not being allowed to satisfy the craving – that's the torture. Smokers will willingly give a cigarette to a complete stranger, but their last cigarette? No way!

That torture of not being able to get your fix of nicotine is not physical, it's purely mental, but it's still real and how do you know when or if it will ever end?

So it follows that smoking is exceedingly difficult to 'give up', doesn't it?

NO IT DOESN'T!

Let's take a closer look at the 'willpower' method. It starts with a feeling of doom and gloom, desperately hoping that, provided we have sufficient willpower, we can endure the misery long enough to be free.

Smokers will willingly give a cigarette to a complete stranger, but their last cigarette? No way!

But why should we be miserable?

After all, we decided that we no longer wanted to smoke. Why aren't we over the moon because we don't have to?

Perhaps you feel it's because of that panic feeling we've been discussing. But that doesn't explain it. We've already established that smokers only get that panic feeling when they want to smoke but aren't allowed to. So why should you get it when you've decided that you *never want to smoke again*?

Perhaps you believe it is because nicotine is an addictive drug, and that the addict has no choice but to continue to crave the drug for an indefinite period after abstention.

This sounds very logical, but doesn't explain anything. What does 'craving' mean? In this context it means nothing more or less than, 'I want a cigarette!' But I've just decided that I never, ever want another, so why am I still craving one? In fact, it's completely illogical.

'I started smoking at 13 and quit at 31 after reading Allen Carr's book. That was 15 months ago now and I am still a happy non-smoker! I have no desire to smoke, nor will I ever again. I have my health, wealth and energy back, which were all taken from me, and I feel great!!!'

Sam H, Australia

Imagine this conversation between two friends over a coffee:

I'd love to come shopping with you on a Saturday, Jane.

I'd really love you to join me, Emma. I hate shopping alone.

But I have to watch John play soccer. It's so boring. He's too old anyway and I just stand there in the wind and rain, terrified that he'll break his leg. And that's the best part! The worst is having to listen to those childish songs after the match.

Well, it's high time he grew up. And you're just as bad for encouraging him.

You're absolutely right, of course. I keep threatening to let him get on with it alone. I've made up my mind – I'm coming shopping with you!

Now try to imagine Emma, the following Saturday, miserably dragging herself from shop to shop, saying:

Sorry, Jane, but I've got this terrible urge to rush over to the game. I'm desperately trying not to give in to it. I hope I don't have to go through this torture every Saturday.

You must have heard smokers say, 'That's it! I'm completely sick of this horrible, filthy habit. I'm spending a fortune just for the privilege of destroying myself. I'm "giving up"!'

Free yourself

According to the American Lung Association, around one in five of the US population smokes. The number of smokers in the European Union is just under a third of the population. The percentage of smokers who want to stop in both territories is well over 90%.

Don't they then go ahead and spend the next few hours, days and weeks saying, 'I could murder for a cigarette!'?

Maybe you've been through this completely illogical process yourself. I did on numerous occasions. 'Addiction' is just a word we use to describe it. But using that word does not explain why otherwise intelligent people act so stupidly.

Give up giving up

You might have noticed that I always put inverted commas round 'give up', and that I only use this expression when I'm referring to a 'willpower' method. This is because the very expression 'give up' implies sacrifice. There is no sacrifice involved in Easyway. You are 'giving up' nothing and gaining everything.

Smokers might dislike being smokers and think it illogical that breathing filthy and lethal fumes into their lungs can be pleasurable, or can help them to concentrate, or can relieve boredom or stress, but the fact is that all of them believe that they get some pleasure or a crutch from smoking.

They don't bother trying to understand why. As far as they're concerned, it's just the case.

All smokers believe they get some pleasure or a crutch from smoking

It seems indisputable that when smokers light up, they feel more relaxed and less distressed than they did the moment before. But if you believe this to be so before you put out what you hope will be your final cigarette, why should you stop believing it after you've finished it?

When the phone rings or the tension is high, your brainwashed mind will continue to urge you to light up. And when your friends smoke after a meal and you are not allowed to, you're going to feel that it is you who is missing out.

You hope that time will solve the problem, but why should it? Doesn't absence just make the heart grow fonder?

'Smoker's breath? It doesn't affect me at all.'

Complaining stoppers

There are some people who succeed in 'giving up' with the 'willpower' method. Some of them will even enthuse about being non-smokers and will tell you genuinely that they don't miss smoking in the slightest. Time solves their problem.

However, of this small minority who succeed in 'giving up', the majority will admit that they do still miss the 'special' cigarette, like the one after a meal.

It is these complaining stoppers who make the rest of us frightened to try stopping, by creating the myth that 'once a smoker, always a smoker' and you can never be completely free.

'Willpower' methods are so difficult for most smokers and impossible for others because we've been brainwashed from birth to believe that they are so difficult.

If you do pluck up enough courage to try one of these methods, the attempt, far from exploding the belief, simply confirms it to be true.

However, the main difficulty with the 'willpower' method is the sheer doubt and uncertainty. We start off hoping, rather than believing or knowing, that we will succeed. This is negative thinking.

Learning to swim can be a difficult and frightening process, but have you ever witnessed the euphoria of a child who has just learned? It might only have been a couple of yards, but that child knows with absolute certainty that she remained afloat under her own steam, without assistance. She can swim!

Influencing others

When you do succeed with Easyway, you will naturally want to help your smoking friends benefit from it. Don't become frustrated if they don't seem too enthused. If they have recently failed a 'willpower' attempt, to ask them to try Easyway would be like trying to persuade a marathon runner who has collapsed a hundred yards short of the finish line to take half an hour's rest and then start all over again.

If your objective is to go a whole year without smoking, it follows that you cannot possibly succeed before the year is up.

If your objective is to go your whole life without a cigarette, it follows that you cannot possibly succeed before your life is up.

Think about what that means.

Even if you do succeed, you won't live to know it!

The other great drawback of the 'willpower' method is that the smokers using it believe they are making a genuine sacrifice. They genuinely believe that they get some pleasure and/or crutch from smoking. All it takes is just one careless or drunken moment and they find themselves back in the trap.

In the previous chapter I asked you to give some thought to the question: 'How do you know when you have succeeded?' I have just implied that it is impossible for anyone to be certain that they will never smoke until their life has ended. So how could anyone who quits with Easyway know they will never smoke again?

'I only smoke when I feel like it. Trouble is, I feel like it most of the time.'

In search of certainty

If you asked a trapper, 'Can you state categorically that you will never get your foot caught in a bear trap?' the answer would probably be 'no'. But change the question slightly. 'Could you state categorically that you will never DELIBERATELY get your foot caught in a bear trap?'

A trapper might go through life in fear of accidentally stepping on a bear trap, but no way does he worry about deliberately doing so, particularly if he once fell into the trap!

Perhaps you find this comparison of the bear trap and smoking unconvincing. It is if you compare it with smokers who are trying to stop using a 'willpower' method. If they are miserable and suspect that the misery is permanent, they might well choose to smoke again.

In fact, over 90 per cent of them do.

But imagine feeling an incredible sense of release and escape – the utter joy of freedom. *Do you think you would worry about getting hooked again?*

CHAPTER 6

Devastation

- *Let me tell you about this new drug.*
- *It's called 'Devastation'.*
- *It comes from a plant that belongs to the same genus as Deadly Nightshade.*
- *It is one of the most addictive drugs known to mankind.*
- *Just one dose will get you hooked.*
- *Over 60 per cent of the adult natives of the tribes who use this drug become hooked.*
- *It is also a powerful poison and is used commercially as an insecticide.*
- *It gradually breaks down the immune system, causes breathlessness and lethargy and kills one in three users.*
- *It tastes bad and systematically destroys the nervous system, causing a feeling of insecurity and lack of confidence.*
- *It costs the addict an average £100,000 ($160,000) over a lifetime.*
- *For that they get... absolutely nothing.*

'You know me. I'll try anything once.'

Now, can I tempt you to try it?

> 'Allen Carr knocks down every excuse for continuing to smoke. Easy read and great results.'
> *Nunya B, USA*

Even the most adventurous, fearless or stupid of us wouldn't take the smallest experimental dose of a drug like Devastation if we believed it would get us hooked.

But supposing you were conditioned from birth into believing that the drug had distinct advantages, and that the downside only took effect if you became addicted, and that, far from one dose hooking you, it took years?

You might just try it.

Now imagine you were hooked and could see all the devastating effects. If you then discovered a method that would release you immediately, easily and permanently, would you hesitate to use it?

And if it worked, would you deliberately step into the trap again?

Read the description of Devastation again and try not to relate it to smoking.

If you then discovered a method that would release you immediately, easily and permanently, would you hesitate to use it?

Do you believe for one second you'd continue to crave cigarettes if the following were true of you?

- You could perceive smoking purely as the drug I have described.
- You knew that smoking did the opposite of relaxing you, helping your concentration, giving you courage and confidence or relieving stress and boredom.
- You knew that in order to escape all you had to do was never to light another cigarette.
- That whenever the subject of smoking entered your head, you thought, 'Eureka! I've kicked it! I'm free!' and not 'I'd love a cigarette' or 'When will I be free?'

When you see smoking as it is and know there is absolutely nothing to give up, only marvellous benefits to receive, you won't have a feeling of doom or gloom or sacrifice.

So why don't I just explain the mystique of addiction and get on with it? Because at this stage you wouldn't believe

A poisoned chalice

If any smoker were to list all the advantages and disadvantages of being a smoker, the disadvantages would far outweigh the advantages. So why, when our rational side tells us we shouldn't smoke, do we continue to do it? The answer? Addiction!

the explanation unless I first removed your doubts. In order to do that I must prove the fallacy of the 'established' facts about smoking, which we are brainwashed from birth to believe.

But there is a more pressing question that we must address first.

If it can work for **any** smoker, why doesn't Easyway work for **every** smoker?

Abracadabra
A good conjuror can mystify us and make his tricks seem like magic. But once a trick is explained, the mystique disappears. The beautiful truth is that there is no nectar in the chalice.

There's not a smoker in history who has received some genuine crutch or pleasure from smoking

CHAPTER 7

Why doesn't Easyway work for every smoker?

Imagine yourself as a teenager wandering into a large public garden and finding it so nice that you don't want to leave. As the years pass you begin to suspect that the fruit in the garden, which you've been living off, has been poisoning you.

You are not too concerned, even though the effects of the poisoning are apparent in many of the other people who live in the garden.

They all appear to be reasonably intelligent, just like you. Occasionally, some do leave, but the vast majority of them choose to return sooner or later.

Eventually you decide you too would like to leave. You discover that the garden is a giant maze and the only exit is also the only entrance.

In order to escape you need to guess the correct path at every junction. The odds against you getting this right are a million to one.

You try, make one mistake and remain in the maze. You try again.

The big problem is you don't know where exactly you made your mistake. You just wander around getting nowhere, not knowing how many decisions you are getting right or wrong.

Eventually you decide there is no point in even trying.

Does the analogy remind you of a smoker using a 'willpower' method to stop? It is, in fact, very similar.

Now suppose there was a map of the maze that showed the path out. You would probably think, 'If I had this map, escape would be easy.'

'The funny thing is, half the time I barely notice I'm smoking.'

But what if this map, although written by trusted experts, gave the wrong information at each junction? Rather than helping you to escape, it would actually ensure you remained trapped.

How much do you know about smoking?

Smokers, together with the 'experts' who advise them, believe they know all there is to know about smoking. Let's put that knowledge to the test. I would like you to respond to the following questionnaire **as you believe the majority of people would respond to it**, and answer 'yes' or 'no' as appropriate. Don't worry about what you personally believe; put that aside.

It's not a taxing questionnaire and I won't be marking your answers. Just give it your best shot.

Questionnaire

1. Do smokers smoke because they choose to?

2. Do people smoke out of habit?

3. Are long-term smokers more hooked than teenagers?

4. Are heavy smokers more hooked than casual smokers?

5. Do youngsters start smoking to feel adult, cool or rebellious?

6. Are smokers stupid?

7. Do smokers enjoy the taste of some cigarettes?

8. Do some cigarettes – e.g. after a meal – taste better than others?

9. Does smoking help to relieve boredom?

10. Does smoking help you to concentrate?

Continued over…

11. Does smoking help you to relax?

12. Does smoking help to relieve stress?

13. Do smokers enjoy smoking?

14. Do some people have addictive personalities?

15. Does smoking help to reduce weight?

16. Does it take willpower to stop?

17. Does it help to use nicotine gum, patches or sprays?

18. Is it necessary to suffer from physical withdrawal symptoms?

19. Do ex-smokers have to endure an initial period of craving and irritability?

20. Is it difficult to stop?

No doubt your answers are a mixture of Yeses and Nos. Astonishingly, the correct answer to all of these questions is:

NO

I claim that Easyway will enable 100 per cent of smokers to stop easily, immediately and permanently.

So why don't 100 per cent succeed?

Because it is not easy for all smokers to understand and/ or to follow all the instructions. Even if you take only one wrong turn, you will remain in the maze.

To ignore one or more of my instructions will not necessarily prevent you from quitting smoking, or even from finding it easy to stop, but it will make it less easy and enjoyable and render you more likely to fall into the trap again.

'Another? Thanks, just one can't do any harm.'

With Easyway, **you cannot fail if you follow all of the instructions**. Don't worry, the instructions are all simple and there are only a few to follow while you read the book.

The first and most challenging is:

KEEP AN OPEN MIND

'I just need to think about quitting to reach for a packet of cigarettes.'

Not bad, eh? Are you thinking, 'If that's the most difficult instruction, this is going to be a doddle!'

If so, beware! You might already be doomed to fail.

Don't underestimate the brainwashing. It is powerful.

Who isn't open-minded?

Try asking your friends if they are open-minded. See if any of them say no. You must have noticed how incredibly biased and prejudiced everybody else in the world is. Isn't it incredible that it's only you and I who are completely open-minded, never jump to conclusions and wouldn't dream of making a judgement without knowing all the facts and hearing both sides of the story?

Some people believe that Easyway is just an exercise in positive thinking. It is more than that. In spite of our attempts to think positively, we fail to 'give up' smoking because we are still using 'willpower' methods.

Ask yourself if you have to use a positive outlook not to inject yourself with heroin. Isn't it more realistic to say you simply don't want these things and never will?

The second instruction is:

MAINTAIN A HAPPY FRAME OF MIND THROUGHOUT

Remember that you are in the enviable position of having a great deal to gain and absolutely nothing to lose. The worst that can happen is that you don't succeed, in which case you will have lost nothing.

Regard Easyway as an exciting challenge: to achieve what every smoker on the planet secretly longs for:

To escape from nicotine slavery

The third instruction is:

MAKE NO ATTEMPT TO STOP OR CUT DOWN BEFORE FINISHING THE BOOK

Of course if you have already stopped smoking, and have not smoked for a day or so, just confirm at the end of this book that you have smoked your final cigarette. If you are using nicotine patches, gum or e-cigarettes, continue to use them until the Final Cigarette ritual at the end of the book. That's when to use, or dispose of, your last patch, piece of gum or e-cigarette.

Your fourth instruction is:

HAVE PATIENCE: DON'T JUMP THE GUN

Read the book in the sequence in which it has been written. Resist the temptation to skip ahead. By all means go back to previous passages to re-read, refresh your memory or clear up any doubts. As you re-read the instructions, ask yourself, 'Am I really following this instruction or just going through the motions?' The reason why Easyway doesn't work for every smoker is simple:

They fail to follow the instructions.

Read all the instructions and make sure you understand and follow them. There is only one more to come and they are not that difficult or complicated. All you have to do to obtain the feeling of euphoria is to follow them.

I don't make it easy to stop smoking. The beautiful truth is that it *is* easy to stop smoking. This is fact. All I do is give you a set of instructions to explain how you too can find it easy to stop.

'I can keep smoking while reading this book? Are you serious?'

The fifth instruction is:

RECORD YOUR PERSONAL STATEMENT

Every smoker is confined in the same prison. The key to release from this prison is to remove the brainwashing. The object of Easyway is to remove the brainwashing of every smoker.

But just as there are actual differences, and distorted differences, between men and women, so each smoker has to contend with his or her individual brainwashing. So pause for a moment and record your own feelings about smoking: what you think it does for you, why you smoke and why you want to stop. This is your Personal Statement.

Keep it handy.

The key
Smokers need to understand they are in a trap before they can get free.
Escape is easy once they are given the key, which is the removal of brainwashing from their minds.

The simplicity of the nicotine trap has been confused out of all proportion and it now appears to be incredibly complicated

As you read the book and we gradually remove the brainwashing, add to your Personal Statement any points that really hit home, and record the page number on which these appear.

The simplicity of the nicotine trap has been confused out of all proportion and it now appears to be incredibly complicated. The mass of society, including the so-called 'experts', perpetuates these illusions and misconceptions, mostly inadvertently.

Smoke and mirrors

A good conjuror will never reveal the key to his trick. Why? Because if he does the trick loses its mystique, the illusion is lost and you are left wondering how you were fooled by it in the first place. It's exactly the same with the nicotine trap. Once it's been revealed for what it is, it is incredibly simple to comprehend and you will never fall for it again. In other words, you will lose your desire to smoke permanently.

We believe them.

Before I can ask you to believe the true and simple explanation of the nicotine trap, I need first to convince you that the facts we have been brainwashed with since birth **cannot** be true.

If the correct answer to each question of the questionnaire is 'no', it follows that smokers get no genuine pleasure or support from smoking. It also means that it would not be difficult for any smoker to stop.

All smokers are aware that there are considerable disadvantages to smoking.

If I could show you categorically that not only does smoking provide no pleasure or support whatsoever, but also that it is a major cause of stress and boredom and actually impedes relaxation and concentration, I think you will see that quitting smoking would indeed be not only easy but enjoyable.

Smoking is a major cause of stress and boredom

CHAPTER 8

The brainwashing

In the interests of open-mindedness, rather than proving that the 'facts' society accepts are definitely wrong, I want you to consider whether these 'facts' are definitely right.

It's a habit

Smoking only becomes a habit *because* people smoke and not the other way around. Anyway, we make and break habits every day of our lives. Habits are easy to break. We don't smoke out of habit.

Smokers do it for pleasure

The reason most smokers can remember their first experimental cigarette is because it tasted bad and made them cough and feel sick. Pleasure did not come into it.

Youngsters suffer the illusion that smokers are enjoying themselves, and that obscures their own natural aversion to the awful taste. By believing in the illusion, they are being hooked just as surely as a fish nibbling at bait.

Perhaps you think smoking is simply an acquired pleasure. But why would you bother to acquire it? Do you remember how hard you worked at smoking? When you started, you almost had to force yourself to do it.

Smoking is a personal choice

Can you remember when you consciously chose to become a permanent smoker? When exactly did you decide to smoke every day and become anxious/uptight/fidgety if you didn't have cigarettes on you?

We no more choose to become smokers than we choose to speak our native tongue. Smoking is just part of the culture we are brought up in. When did you actually decide that you'd have to smoke day in, day out and never be able to stop?

'Well, if I didn't choose to smoke, what made me start?'

If we had a choice, why would we find it so difficult to stop? Why would you need to read this book? We aren't smoking out of choice but because we *aren't able to exercise our choice*.

We are caught in a trap from which we don't know how to escape.

But there are no iron bars and there's no jailer. Once you discover the key to your escape, you will enjoy exercising your choice to use it immediately and permanently

Nobody chooses to become a smoker. Sadly, most of us dabble at one time or another, and sadder still, most of us get hooked.

The longer you smoke, the harder it is to quit

The facts don't bear this out: it's the longer-term, heavier smokers who are stopping, not the younger, casual smokers.

Who is more effectively hooked, the person who believes they smoke out of choice or the person who believes they are trapped?

'I'd die without my post-Pilates puff!'

Unless you realize that you are in a trap, you'll have no desire to escape from it. And if you have no desire to stop, your chances of stopping smoking are zero.

Unless you realise that you are in a trap, you'll have no desire to escape from it

Some cigarettes are special

How can an identical cigarette out of the very same packet taste different just because of the occasion? It's purely the brainwashing that makes you believe that some cigarettes taste better than others.

Cigarettes help smokers to function

No one needs to smoke to help them function before they fall into the trap. It's only smokers who can't relax, concentrate, enjoy a meal or answer the phone without a cigarette.

How can a cigarette relieve boredom and stress and also assist concentration and relaxation? Boredom and concentration are opposites, as are stress and relaxation.

Behind the contradictions

Why do we accept these obvious contradictions? And why do we do so even when we are fully aware that our little friend or support is incredibly expensive and has awful side-effects?

Only the most stupid parents on the planet would fail to discourage their children from smoking. Parents who smoke will do so more vehemently than parents who have never smoked. Yet those same parents will spend hours telling you about the pleasure or support they get from smoking.

It's because all smokers sense that they really smoke because they have fallen into a trap, not because they choose to.

Suck it and see

If you believe that cigarettes taste marvellous and that smoking is enjoyable, put it to the test. Light one up now. Take six deep inhalations and ask yourself what it is that you are actually enjoying. Concentrate on every single aspect of the cigarette in your hand as it goes to your mouth and you breathe in the smoke.

If, when you come to stop, you still believe that you get some pleasure from smoking, then you'll go on believing it. Once you know you get no pleasure from it, then you know you won't be missing it for the rest of your life.

Enjoyment would disappear if you were conscious of what smoking does to you

The illusion of enjoyment would disappear if, every time you smoked, you were conscious:

- of breathing unhealthy fumes into your lungs
- that this might just be the one cigarette to trigger cancer in you
- that it was going to cost you a small fortune in your lifetime.

But the truth is we smoke the vast majority of cigarettes without even being conscious of how they taste or what they're doing to us. This explains the double standards.

As a woman passes through her life she will use the excuses pertinent to her at a particular stage to continue smoking, and all the while her smoker friends will be there to reinforce the excuses.

WHEN A RELATIONSHIP FAILS, CIGARETTES ARE USED AS CONSOLATION.

WHEN THE STRESSES AND STRAINS IN LIFE AND WORK SURFACE, CIGARETTES ARE THERE APPARENTLY TO REPRESENT TIME OUT.

WHEN THE BODY IS GOING THROUGH THE NATURAL CHANGES OF LIFE, WOMEN SMOKERS WILL SWEAR THAT CIGARETTES HELP TO RESTORE HORMONAL BALANCE.

These are excuses and excuses they will remain. Excuses that mask the real truth. After all, who wants to stand among their peers and declare that they feel miserable and have come to the conclusion:

I'M A FOOL! I MUST STOP DOING IT!

Feeling more receptive?

I haven't at this point proved that smokers get no pleasure or support from smoking. But hopefully you will have opened your mind and will agree that the 'facts' society has brainwashed us to believe about smoking just don't add up.

These 'facts' amount to confusion, contradiction and cliché. Even a cursory examination reveals this. It's time now to determine the truth about nicotine addiction.

A smoker who has run out of excuses faces an even more frightening spectre: the fear of 'giving up' and of life without cigarettes. So she compromises: 'I will give up, but not today.'

The fact never seems to occur to us:

There will <u>never</u> be a good time to 'give up'.

This is one of the ingenuities, not only of the nicotine trap but of all drug addiction: it is designed to keep you trapped for life.

'WOW, WOW, WOW!
I'm a non-smoker. I would recommend Allen Carr's Easyway to anyone who wants to be free of the disgusting, poisonous addiction!
Thank you so much'
Jamie L, Finland

CHAPTER 9

Nicotine addiction

Nicotine comes from the tobacco plant, which is a relative of Deadly Nightshade. It is a powerful poison, used commercially as an insecticide.

Scientists who handle it in laboratories wear anti-contamination suits, not dissimilar to those used in the handling of nuclear waste.

If you were to inject the nicotine content of just one cigarette directly into a vein, you would die.

(Please take my word for this and on no account test it out.)

Nicotine is by far the most powerfully addictive drug known to mankind. At one time more than 80 per cent of the adult male population in the Western world was addicted to nicotine. Its power lies in its speed, the rate at which it enters the body. Thankfully it also leaves the body incredibly quickly, and almost imperceptibly... and that ironically is also its weakness.

5,000,000 – that's the number of people who die annually as a result of nicotine addiction. That's the equivalent of more than 10,000 jumbo jets crashing out of the sky every year, a rate of nearly 30 plane crashes a day. It might surprise you to learn that this figure has been increasing every year. The World Health Organization estimates that by the 2020s the number of deaths will be in excess of 10 million yearly.

Every puff on a cigarette delivers a small dose of nicotine that acts more rapidly than a dose of heroin injected directly into a vein.

If it takes you 20 puffs to smoke a cigarette, with just one cigarette you take 20 shots of nicotine.

0 minutes – as soon as the cigarette is put out the nicotine starts to leave the body rapidly and the smoker begins to experience withdrawal symptoms.

30 minutes – within just half an hour of extinguishing a cigarette, levels of nicotine in the bloodstream drop by half.

1 hour – within an hour, three-quarters of the nicotine has left the body.

The physical symptoms of withdrawal from nicotine are so slight as to be hardly noticeable.

Immediately after lighting the next cigarette, the nicotine is replaced and the empty, insecure feeling disappears. This creates the feeling that smokers describe as enjoyable, satisfying or relaxing. In fact, it's nothing more than relief – rather like removing a pair of tight shoes. It's actually fake relief. After all, you wouldn't wear tight shoes just for the 'relief' when you take them off.

I usually refer to that empty, insecure feeling of withdrawal as the 'little monster'. Although it's a genuine physical aggravation, it is so imperceptible as to be hardly noticeable.

'My world's revolved around cigarettes for far too long.'

Just about every smoker has lived and died without even realizing that the 'little monster' exists – nor that the only reason they light up is to try to feed its insatiable appetite.

Before Copernicus, everyone on the planet believed that the Sun moves round the Earth. Now we know it was an illusion created by one simply explained misconception.

Even today, we still visualize the situation as the Sun rising in the east and setting in the west, rather than the Earth spinning on its own axis. But we know what the truth is.

I refer to that empty, insecure feeling as the 'little monster'

> 'I wanted to thank you for saving my life! I have been cigarette-free for 2 years and I will NEVER EVER smoke again.'
> *Luisa, Mexico*

The nicotine trap is not so simple to see through, for several reasons.

1. The 'little monster' is just a feeling and, although you can see the effects of a feeling, the feeling itself is invisible.
2. The feeling itself is almost imperceptible.
3. The feeling is indistinguishable from normal hunger and insecurity.
4. It works back to front. It is when we are NOT smoking that the 'little monster' starts to nag us to light up.

Back to front

This reverse effect is the key to all drug addiction. Someone who has never been addicted to heroin would be horrified to watch an addict self-inject with the drug. It is blatantly obvious to the onlooker that the addict is not doing it to obtain wonderful hallucinations but to relieve the misery of withdrawal.

Although it is the first dose that hooks us, the whole addiction process is usually so gradual that it can take years for us to realize that we are hooked.

The process

A typical cigarette contains about 9 mg of nicotine, but 90 per cent of this burns away, meaning a smoker absorbs less than 1 mg. Nicotine attaches itself to the tar in smoke, which coats the lung tissue and slowly destroys it.

The truth only hits us when we try to stop and find we can't. Even then it doesn't really sink in. Instead we begin to make excuses. 'I picked a bad time,' is a favourite.

Addiction is rather like growing old: it happens so gradually we don't notice it. But study a photo of yourself taken ten years ago and the change is alarming.

A picture of euphoria

I would love to be able to show you a snapshot of how you will feel, both physically and emotionally, three weeks after extinguishing your final cigarette. You'll be thinking, 'Will I really feel this good?' Unfortunately, I can't project into your future – but you can. All you have to do is open your mind, follow the instructions and use your imagination.

With nicotine addiction, we forget that we were able to enjoy social occasions, concentrate and cope with stress before we got hooked. Even when our lethargic state becomes obvious, we blame it on ageing rather than our little 'friend'.

There is one more ingenious aspect to the nicotine trap and that is the devious way it uses our own protective mechanisms against us.

If something smells bad, it's poison. If it tastes bad, it's poison

Mother Nature has given all creatures two ingenious devices for self-protection: smell and taste. If something smells bad, it's poison. If you are not sure, sample a morsel. If it tastes bad, it's poison. The system is so ingenious that even if good food turns putrid, it will smell and taste repellent.

This is why our first cigarettes taste awful. Our body is telling us, 'You are feeding me poison, please don't!' The lucky ones, for whatever reason, heed the warning and never smoke again.

If we don't heed the warnings, Mother Nature gives us a second chance by making us cough and feel increasingly giddy and nauseous. Many of us heed her warning and never smoke again, but others are determined to carry on regardless.

If we continue to smoke on a regular basis, she assumes that we do so because we have no choice, not because we are stupid enough to choose to. Ironically, her assumption is correct.

'I'll try to give up just as soon as I get rid of this dreadful cough.'

She then triggers yet another survival mechanism that is a miracle in itself. But while it protects us, it also adds to the effectiveness of the nicotine trap. I'm talking about our immune system.

Many people believe that coughing and nausea are themselves diseases. On the contrary, they are two highly ingenious survival devices with which Mother Nature has equipped us to eject poisons from our lungs and other parts of the body.

CHAPTER 10

The danger of immunity

By far the most powerful and effective healing force available to mankind – or indeed any species – is our immune system.

It not only fights disease but is so sophisticated that if you continue to poison your body on a regular basis, it will build a partial immunity to the poison.

When we teach ourselves to smoke tobacco regularly, we build an immunity to the bad taste and poisonous effects. In case you are now thinking, 'Great! My immune system will prevent me from contracting lung cancer, emphysema, arteriosclerosis or any of the other killer diseases', bear in mind that you not only build an immunity to the poisonous effects of the drug, which is only partial anyway, but you also build immunity to the drug itself.

Therefore you automatically start taking more of the drug. Smokers generally do this by smoking more cigarettes as they get older and/or taking bigger drags on each cigarette and/or holding each drag in their lungs for a bit longer.

When we teach ourselves to smoke tobacco regularly, we build an immunity to the bad taste and poisonous effects

Rasputin was able to survive a dose of arsenic 20 times greater than the dose that would kill an average human being. This was because he took small amounts over time that enabled him to build his immunity to it.

When we put out that very first cigarette, the nicotine will begin to leave our body and we will experience withdrawal. At this stage the empty, insecure feeling is so slight that we aren't even aware of it. All we feel is slightly unwell.

If we light another cigarette the nicotine will be replaced and the empty, insecure feeling will go.

We will feel the same as we did before we lit that first cigarette.

'I smoke to feel like a non-smoker? I need to think about that.'

Stop and think about that for a moment. This is a mind-blowing concept. It means that the only reason smokers continue to smoke is to feel like they did before they lit their first cigarette. So the pleasure or crutch that smokers talk about is nothing more than

FEELING LIKE A NON-SMOKER.

Pleasure vs addiction

I love lobster but I can go years without eating it and it doesn't bother me in the least. I don't feel insecure or get into a panic. This is how you can tell the difference between genuine pleasure and drug addiction. With smoking there is a chain effect. Each cigarette creates the need for the next.

The pleasure or crutch feeling is real, but it is an illusion to believe that the cigarette should take the credit for it. On the contrary, the cigarette was responsible for the discomfort in the first place.

To claim that cigarettes relax you is like claiming that tight shoes relax you

To claim that cigarettes relax you is like claiming that tight shoes relax you. At least when you take off tight shoes, the relief is permanent, provided you don't put them on again.

When you smoke a cigarette, you are actually creating a new wave of discomfort by putting more nicotine into your body.

In fact, smoking that second cigarette does not make us feel quite the same as we did before the first. This is because of our immune system.

As our body builds immunity to nicotine, we find that we don't quite get back to par when we light up again. We live with a permanent nicotine hangover, a state of discomfort which we believe is normal.

'Hangover? A few more of these and I'll feel right as rain.'

Like all other forms of drug addiction, the tendency is to light up more often, which simply perpetuates the process.

The fly trap

Getting hooked is like a fly being slowly trapped in a pitcher plant. When it first lands on the plant and starts to sample the nectar, the fly thinks nothing of the dangers. It keeps feeding, moving further into the plant. By the time it decides that it wants to leave, it is already stuck and soon realizes that it is being devoured by the plant, not vice versa. For the smoker, this moment of realization is what I call the 'critical point'. You're there already. That's why you're reading this book.

'Well, what else are hands for?'

Observe smokers who have gone longer than usual without being able to light up. They begin to get restless and fidgety, playing with their lighters or tapping their packet of cigarettes.

Eventually their hands will go up to their mouths and they will start to tense their jaw muscles.

It's this feeling that smokers describe as needing to do something with their hands. Non-smokers don't have this problem.

Reaching the 'critical point' is like being pulled in half. One part of your brain wants you to smoke more and more, another wants you to smoke less and less. You are now in the unenviable position of not being allowed to smoke enough and yet smoking too much. From this point on you will not suffer even the illusion of enjoying being a smoker.

During sessions at our clinics there usually comes a time when nobody has lit up for a while and no one wants to be the first to do so. The clients tend to become restless and their hands go to their mouths. I stop what I am saying and point out that they are all now obviously restless. I do this for two very good reasons:

1. To make them see the truth – that it's not so much that smokers are relaxed when they are smoking as that they are decidedly **unrelaxed** when they aren't.
2. Not only are they becoming restless, they are clearly no longer concentrating.

This is another reason why I'd like you to continue to smoke until you've finished reading the book. I don't want you sitting there restless and agitated. I want you to be relaxed and absorbing the truths that I am explaining.

Is this an admission that smoking helps you to relax and concentrate?

On the contrary. It is proof that smoking impedes relaxation and concentration.

> 'I think about smoking but only because I am proud of myself to have stopped and cannot get over it.'
> *Joanne H, UK*

CHAPTER 11

The 'big monster'

The good news is that you are never severely addicted to the drug itself. The 'little monster' is simply part of the overall illusion. The catalyst that creates the real problem is what we call the 'big monster'.

The 'big monster' is the brainwashing. It is the belief in all the illusions about relaxation, concentration, social occasions etc.

The only reason that some smokers don't succeed with Easyway is because they fail to follow all the instructions. The main reason they don't follow the instructions is because they take the advice of a doctor or some other so-called 'expert'.

Seeing the light at last!

I have been accused of being arrogant. The accusations don't bother me too much. I have valid reasons for appearing to be. My insistence that I am right and all the so-called 'experts' are wrong is born of frustration. It is only now, more than a quarter of a century since I started Easyway, that increasing numbers of experts are beginning to agree that it is the psychological state of the individual addict that needs to be addressed and not the substance itself.

The effect of withdrawal is an empty, insecure feeling, like having an itch.

The only reason any smoker continues to smoke is to scratch that ‘itch’.

Not because they enjoy smoking...

or because it relaxes them...

or improves meals...

or relieves stress...

or helps them to concentrate.

I didn’t discover that when nicotine leaves the body, smokers suffer an empty, insecure feeling that is relieved when they light another cigarette. Apparently this process had been known by the medical profession and, incidentally, the tobacco industry for years and was simply regarded as one of the reasons smokers found it difficult to stop.

My great discovery was to realize that the need to scratch this itch is the only reason any smoker continues to smoke

It soon became clear that before I could convince any smoker that what I was claiming was true, I had to tackle the 'big monster'. I had to remove the brainwashing and the illusions and show them that what they believed *was not* true.

No one would deliberately place their hands in boiling water just for the relief of removing them. But this is what smokers effectively do.

Once they can see this clearly and understand it, they stop immediately and permanently and are happy to do so.

The frame of mind we are aiming for is not, 'I must never, ever smoke another cigarette.' It is the attitude that someone who has never been addicted to heroin would have towards a heroin addict.

'No-one dictates to me. I have my ciggies to do that.'

'Pity that poor sap! Thank goodness I'm free!'

In order to achieve that frame of mind permanently, you need first to remove the brainwashing and see smoking as it really is: nothing more or less than addiction to Devastation.

CHAPTER 12

What is your favourite perfume?

When it comes to taking pride in one's appearance, women have always put men in the shade. For women it is nothing less than an art form and one to be greatly admired. The clothes, the hair, the make-up, the perfume – it all takes time, money and thought. But all that effort can be completely ruined by breath that smells like an ashtray and hair, fingers and clothes that stink of stale cigarette smoke.

This is one reason why all women smokers begin to despise themselves, even though many of them cannot actually bring themselves to admit it, and none of them can understand why they continue to smoke.

The reason might appear to be rank stupidity, but really it's fear. It's also another demonstration of the incredible power of nicotine addiction.

'It's my brand new perfume. Essence of Ashtray.'

Caught in the act

You may have tried to look the part by standing in front of a mirror and practising how to smoke 'with allure'. But when the lens of a camera or camcorder is focused on you, will you pose, pout or try to smoke sexily? Not on your life! Then it's a frantic, 'Where can I stub out my cigarette?'

While many women are brainwashed into smoking by the 'glamorous' role models they see smoking in films or on television, the truth is that nicotine has a devastating effect on your physical appearance. And it comes from inside.

I'm not referring to nicotine-stained lungs, I am referring to the gradual and cumulative gunging up of all your blood vessels that nicotine causes.

If you knew for certain that the next cigarette would be the one to trigger lung cancer, would you smoke it?

'I desperately wanted to be more glamorous, but smoking made me look and feel terrible.'

> You probably suspect that I'm now using the doctors' method by trying to frighten you into stopping. Not so; that tactic didn't help me to stop and if it would help you, you would already be free.

With smoking, the supply of oxygen and nutrients to every organ, muscle and bone in the body is gradually replaced by carbon monoxide and other poisons.

This results in the dried-up look, or you may notice liver spots on your skin, see specks in front of your eyes whenever you stand up quickly, or develop severe varicose veins. We daren't even think about those dreaded wrinkles that we pass off as laughter lines.

We don't want to attribute the physical changes to smoking and prefer to explain away our appearance by putting it down to natural colouring, a hectic lifestyle or old age. We live in fear of being made to laugh because of the hacking, rasping nature of the noise we involuntarily emit.

The gunging up process also impedes the immune system. It's fighting a never-ending battle against everyday illnesses and diseases, including cancer. If it's defective, it can't do its job properly and must prioritize.

> Our immune system is like a bank; it has finite reserves. Keep taking out and you'll discover, to your great cost, that there is no overdraft facility.

Have you heard those stories about smokers who are warned by their doctors that gangrene will set in and they will have to have their toes amputated if they don't stop? Still they don't stop. They have toes amputated, or even feet or part of a leg. Do you think they choose to have a leg removed rather than stop smoking because of the wonderful pleasure or support they get from it?

Have you ever heard a non-smoker enthuse about how her hair and body smells and how great she feels?

You will know smokers who have managed to stop without the help of Easyway, and possibly some of them found it relatively easy. But do they enthuse about it like Debbie and other ex-smokers who quit with Easway?

You might have noticed that they always refer to 'giving up'. They truly believe that they have made a genuine sacrifice.

With Easyway, we never refer to 'giving up', but to quitting, stopping or, most accurate of all, escaping!

'By the end of the book, I was literally sick at the thought of another cigarette... I'm done with them and couldn't be happier.'
Lora, USA

Unfortunately, stories about smokers being prepared to die rather than 'give up' reinforce two of the most stubbornly held beliefs about smoking:

1. That cigarettes are providers of great pleasure and/or a crutch.
2. That nicotine addiction exerts an unshakeable hold over its victims.

The natural conclusion is:

'If a smoker threatened with limb amputation still cannot stop, how can Allen Carr expect me to believe that any smoker can find it easy to stop and that no smoker need suffer from severe nicotine withdrawal symptoms?'

Don't be concerned: I only have good news for you!

CHAPTER 13

Hunger

Because of brainwashing, hunger is a feeling that's more familiar to women in general than to men. For decades women have been targeted with images of the 'ideal' body and 'desired look'.

Much food is now designed for 'convenience'. Much of the food we consume looks good, fills our bellies and tastes good too. It also happens to be laden with additives, sugar and salt.

It is 'short-change' food. The manufacturing process it undergoes strips it of the natural energy and nutrients we require.

The poor return leaves our bodies in need – perpetually hungry. Our response to the constant 'I'm hungry' signals is to eat more processed food, which promptly turns to fat.

'Don't mind if I do. This should make up for missing breakfast.'

You might believe that the only food that is good for you tastes like cardboard. Actually, the foods that benefit you most taste the best. (If you find that hard to believe, read *Lose Weight Now, The Easyweigh to Lose Weight* or *No More Diets*.)

Some women spend much of their lives dieting in order to maintain their figures and/or fitness and health. Most diets starve the body of the nutrients it needs. The result of this is hunger. And the inevitable result of hunger is eating.

We tend to regard hunger as a terrible evil. It isn't. It is just another of Mother Nature's ingenious devices to ensure that we survive whether we like it or not. In the wild, it is the signal that tells animals when it's time to eat.

Humans are no different.

If you eat nutritious meals at regular times, you won't be hungry until your next meal is due.

'Got this book as a gag gift from a friend. Wasn't planning on giving up. Read the book in two nights and haven't smoked since.'
Mary, Ireland

Even when we are aware of being hungry, there's no actual physical pain

Even when we are aware of being hungry and are unable to satisfy our hunger, there's no actual physical pain. It's just an empty, insecure feeling, which we only know as 'I want to eat'.

If this feeling is not satisfied, it soon becomes 'I must eat'. If food is scarce or unobtainable, fear and panic enter the equation and the feeling becomes 'If I can't obtain food soon, I will die'.

This fear of death brought on by extreme hunger is both real and powerful.

Why nicotine comes first

The craving for nicotine is indistinguishable from a hunger for food but it has a more powerful effect. On average we have to satisfy our hunger for food only three times a day, whereas our craving for nicotine occurs much more frequently. The average 20-a-day smoker will experience this craving some 7,120 times a year. Understandably, our behaviour is geared to getting rid of the discomfort we experience most often. The nicotine itch takes precedence over anything else.

Breakfast is the favourite meal of most non-smokers, simply because the longer you fast the greater the pleasure of eating. Having satisfied their hunger and provided their bodies with the energy and nutrients they need, they no longer have an empty, insecure feeling and are equipped to enjoy the day.

For a 20-a-day smoker to be without nicotine for eight hours is equivalent to a non-smoker being without food for nearly three days

For many smokers, the first cigarette of the day is the one they look forward to most. Why?

Because they have gone 8 hours without smoking.

Although the awful, empty, insecure feeling caused by hunger is indistinguishable from the symptoms of nicotine withdrawal, satisfying one will not satisfy the other.

This creates confusion in the mind of smokers. They wake up with an additional empty, insecure feeling and their first instinct is to light up, no matter how bad that experience might be.

'When I'm hungry I find myself reaching for a cigarette.'

Non-smokers are completely relaxed once they've satisfied their hunger. Smokers continue to feel the empty, insecure feeling. This is why the cigarette after a meal is so important to smokers. It's not that a cigarette enhances a meal for smokers, but that they cannot even enjoy that meal unless and until they can feed the 'little monster'.

Since the craving for nicotine cannot actually be satisfied by smoking a cigarette, it means that a smoker is permanently hungry.

Ironically, the situation becomes even more confusing when smokers attempt to stop by using a 'willpower' method. When they feel genuine hunger after 'giving up', they interpret the empty, insecure feeling as, 'I want or need a cigarette!'

Since we can no longer partially relieve the feeling by smoking, the natural tendency is to reverse the procedure by eating chocolates, sucking boiled sweets or chewing gum.

'Have given up the cigarettes and it has been SO EASY. The little monster is dead. Have not had an urge at all. Glad to be completely free at last. Husband is contemplating reading it now!!!'

Clare D, UK

Eventually your reserves of willpower are exhausted and you find some excuse to light up

These substitutes won't even partially relieve the 'little monster'. What they will do is coat your teeth with sugar, ruin your appetite, make you put on pounds and leave you feeling miserable and frustrated.

You will sense – without understanding why – that the only thing that will help relieve that empty feeling is a cigarette. You won't allow yourself to have one, though, and you will then feel even more deprived and miserable.

Once you understand the nicotine trap, the mystery isn't so much why otherwise strong-willed people cannot 'give up' by using willpower, so much as how any smoker manages to succeed using it.

In fact, only a small percentage of them ever do.

Even those 'willpower' quitters who survive the few days necessary without nicotine for the 'little monster' to die are never sure when they are free. They will interpret genuine hunger as 'I need a cigarette!' for weeks, months or even years.

'Cut off my nicotine supply? How am I going to cope?!!'

You might well be asking yourself how long it takes for the 'little monster' to die, and how will you know when he is dead? These questions are irrelevant.

The 'little monster' is doomed the moment you cut off its supply of nicotine.

Perhaps you are worrying about suffering during the period that our bodies continue to experience that empty, insecure feeling after cutting off the supply of nicotine.

Remember, smokers experience that feeling throughout their smoking lives and it is so slight they don't even realize that it exists.

It's only the lack of understanding that causes the confusion and frustration. Once you realize that the empty feeling is caused by the previous cigarette and the one thing that will prevent its relief is another cigarette, that period can be one of exquisite joy rather than misery.

'My mom said,
"No book can help you quit smoking." Well, she was wrong.'
Misty B, USA

It is its similarity to hunger that makes addiction to nicotine such a powerful force.

A closer examination reveals that the similarity is a subtle illusion. In reality the two practices are diametrically opposed.

Food provides health, energy, happiness, and prolongs our life.

Tobacco ruins our health, causes misery and lethargy and shortens our lives.

Food tastes good and satisfying your hunger is a genuinely pleasant experience.

Inhaling cancerous and foul-tasting fumes into your lungs is a decidedly unpleasant experience.

Eating doesn't create hunger, it satisfies it.

Far from satisfying the 'little monster', our first cigarette actually creates it. Each subsequent cigarette that you smoke renews its appetite. The only way to satisfy it is to stop feeding it!

Relax with a cigarette?
Remember, all you actually enjoy when you smoke is getting somewhere near the relaxed state that non-smokers enjoy all the time. Immunity prevents you reaching that relaxed state, even for the few minutes that you are partially relieving those withdrawal symptoms.

A good meal at a nice restaurant is a pleasant ritual; however, its main purpose is to satisfy a natural hunger at a certain time of the day, and it would be unpleasant if you weren't able to satisfy that hunger.

'I'll just have a starter and then I'll pop outside for my main.'

Many smokers say they enjoy the ritual of smoking: the gold lighters, the glossy packaging. But the whole ritual is designed for one object alone: to try to satisfy the 'little monster'.

- That's why we have to light the cigarette.
- That's why we have to stick it in our mouths.
- That's why we breathe the filth into our lungs.

Just to get the nicotine.

The phenomenon of snuff-taking will help you to see cigarette smoking in its true light. You are probably aware that snuff is simply powdered tobacco and was the most common form of nicotine addiction prior to the mass production of cigarettes. It is difficult to believe nowadays that it too was once regarded as a highly sociable pastime.

> If you harbour illusions about switching to roll-ups, small cigars or even a pipe, forget it! They are all devices for taking in nicotine, nothing more, nothing less. Similarly, e-cigarettes are just another way of getting a nicotine fix. But no one knows yet what harm they do. Inhaling nicotine vapour is unlikely to enhance your health.

Snuff addicts carried their drug around in little silver boxes, a glamorous wrapper to conceal a filthy habit. Like cocaine addicts, they sniffed the powder up their noses. They did it to obtain the effects of the drug.

The true reason why any smoker continues to smoke is to end the empty, insecure feeling that the previous cigarette created.

Start thinking of the 'little monster' as an actual monster living inside you, which feeds on nicotine. As it grows it creates more discomfort and the uneasy feeling you experience all the time. You created it with the first cigarette and you've been feeding it ever since.

Start thinking of the 'little monster' as an actual monster living inside you

Once we've removed the brainwashing, you are going to starve it.

'You mean, I don't have to go through cold turkey?!!'

There are some important points to establish about nicotine addiction. Although nicotine is the most powerful addictive drug known to mankind, that only relates to the speed at which it traps its victims. The beautiful truth is:

No smoker is ever badly addicted to nicotine.

Be clear: it is the illusion that hooks us, not the nicotine itself.

Remove the brainwashing from your mind and the addiction is easy to break.

You have no doubt heard that every cigarette takes five minutes off your life and that it takes ten years for the effects to leave your body.

It is the illusion that hooks us, not the nicotine itself

These reports are true, but only if you continue to smoke or have already contracted a terminal disease.

Provided you haven't already done that, you can regain 99 per cent of those lost minutes and you can look forward to returning to great health – almost as if you never smoked in the first place.

We need to overcome the negative ideas that smokers often harbour about what it's like to be a non-smoker. When you're smoking, you convince yourself you're 'enjoying a smoke'. You may wonder, could you ever sit there thinking, 'I'm enjoying not smoking'? The fact is that you will be able to. I do it every day of my life.

Get it clearly into your mind that you are simply stopping smoking:

You don't have to stop living.

I would like you to stop smoking, not because smoking is a filthy, disgusting addiction that is ruining your health and wealth and depriving you of your freedom, or because it is causing distress to your family. I want you to stop for a purely selfish reason:

That you will enjoy life so much more as a non-smoker.

The physical withdrawal from nicotine is almost imperceptible and gets no worse when you put out your final cigarette. It is the illusions that cause the torture.

Fortunately, we can remove the brainwashing before you put out your final cigarette. By the time you do so, provided you have followed all the instructions, you will already be a happy non-smoker.

CHAPTER 14

Happy casual smokers

Heavy smokers find it almost impossible to believe that there is no such being as a happy casual smoker. If you are a casual smoker yourself, you won't be a happy one. If you were happy to be a casual smoker, you wouldn't be reading this book.

All smokers have to lie to themselves and to other people. Because they are usually honest, upright citizens in other matters, they are also people we respect, and so we believe their lies.

Casual smokers claim that they can take them or leave them. But if they genuinely enjoy the taste of a cigarette after a meal or when answering the phone, why would they want to go several days or a whole week without them?

Everyone knows that smoking is the No. 1 killer in the Western world. If casual smokers could genuinely take or leave cigarettes, only a fool would actually take them. Unless, of course, they were hooked.

> Why should heavy smokers envy casual smokers? When I was a golf fanatic playing three times a week, I didn't envy the poor sap who could play only once a week.

When casual smokers brag about their ability to take or leave cigarettes, they are actually trying to convince you and themselves that they do not have a smoking problem. In reality they are admitting the complete opposite.

Casual smokers try to convince themselves they do not have a problem

If they had no problem, there would be no need to make the statement.

Anybody who takes heroin, no matter how infrequently, is not a 'user' but an addict. Exactly the same applies to smokers. Remember, we are talking about Devastation. No one would take that drug if they could genuinely leave it.

The best of both worlds

If you have ever made a successful attempt to cut down, you might remember the self-righteous feeling of those first few days. You had achieved the heavy smoker's dream of paradise: your level of smoking was so low that you no longer had to worry about the expense, or contracting a horrific disease. At the same time, you didn't have to 'give up' completely. You believed you had the best of both worlds. How long did it last?

Mary was a young housewife who had been smoking 40 a day and was trying to stop by cutting down. One afternoon she screwed up her packet of cigarettes in disgust and threw it in the bin. An hour later, she was rummaging through the potato peelings trying to find a cigarette.

The next day she experienced the same revulsion to smoking. She was an intelligent woman and wasn't going to make the same mistake again, so she smeared mustard over the cigarettes before banishing them to the trash. An hour later she was scraping potato peelings and mustard from those cigarettes.

Most smokers have gone through a similar experience in their lives, yet some still insist they smoke only for the marvellous taste.

Mary decided she'd have to ease herself off cigarettes by cutting out just one cigarette each day. After about six weeks she was down to just one a day. But she couldn't bring herself to cut out that last cigarette.

An hour later she was scraping potato peelings and mustard from those cigarettes

All day long, Mary would be dangling the cigarette like a carrot under her own nose. She knew that she wasn't going to smoke it until just before her children came home from school.

Having craved it all day, can you imagine how enjoyable that cigarette must have seemed to her, and what she had to suffer to obtain that illusory pleasure?

Apart from those few minutes while she was actually smoking the cigarette, she spent every waking moment of her day and evening feeling deprived and miserable, obsessed by her need to smoke.

The cigarette tasted just as bad as it always did. Her pleasure was just the temporary ending of the misery of the craving. But that cigarette caused her to suffer the same misery day after day.

'I've been longing for this all day, but am I really enjoying it?'

Had you asked Mary how she was getting on, she would have said, 'I'm doing great! Now I need only one cigarette a day!'

And you would no doubt have envied her.

> Envying a casual smoker is equivalent to envying someone who is forced to spend the whole of their life on a permanent diet, with the added disadvantage that the diet is not food but poison.

The only pleasure in smoking is ending the aggravation of the body craving nicotine. Just like a hunger for food, the longer you suffer it, the more marvellous it will seem when you relieve the suffering.

Mary wasn't removing her illusory dependence on nicotine, but simply ingraining in her mind that the only precious thing on earth is a cigarette.

If you've ever tried cutting down in any of its various forms, you will know this approach only works for a short period.

> If any smoker has actually succeeded in 'giving up' smoking by weaning themselves off cigarettes gradually, I take my hat off to them. They must have phenomenal willpower. At the same time, I can only pity them for the torture they must have inflicted upon themselves.

The lies of casual smokers make us believe that it is possible to cut down. They create the illusion of the happy casual smoker.

The lies of casual smokers make us believe it is possible to cut down

Of the thousands of cigarettes that you must have smoked, how many can you actually remember smoking? How often can you remember inhaling deeply and thinking to yourself, 'This is a gorgeous experience'?

Can you remember once thinking to yourself, 'I'm so pleased I took up smoking. I'm so lucky to be a smoker'? Or did you find yourself just drifting into it like every other smoker, blocking your mind to the reality with a vague promise that you would 'give up' one day, when the time was right?

Dizzy logic

All smokers have a problem explaining the pleasure they get from smoking. Some youngsters will tell you, 'It makes me feel dizzy!' Ask them if they are really prepared to spend a fortune and risk awful diseases just to make themselves feel dizzy, when they can achieve exactly the same effect by closing their eyes and spinning around, and not surprisingly they feel somewhat foolish.

'My favourite cigarette? The next one… that's it, the next one!'

It's human nature that we tend to forget the bad times in our lives and remember the good particularly fondly.

However, when we look back on our smoking lives, it is only the bad times that we are able to recall.

That's why most of us can clearly remember the experience of our very first experimental cigarettes: and not because they were so marvellous, but because they were so foul.

We all have memories of searching for an all-night gas station, because we get into a panic without cigarettes.

And be honest. More than a few of us have smoked the butts out of an ashtray when we've run out – even when the butts haven't been our own!

Most of us think that the cigarette after a meal is very special, but of all the thousands of post-meal cigarettes you've had, can you remember smoking a single one of them?

Yet you'll remember those meals that were ruined for you because you weren't allowed to smoke.

If you believe that you smoke at the level you do because you got into the habit of smoking at that level, then it is logical to assume that it's possible to reverse the process.

Why do so many smokers who gave up using 'willpower' still crave cigarettes?

In other words, if you can discipline yourself to gradually smoke less, soon it will become a habit to smoke less and you won't even want to smoke more.

Continue the process and it will soon become a habit not to need or want a cigarette at all. It's so simple and obvious. So why doesn't it work?

Why are so many smokers who have actually succeeded in 'giving up' when using a 'willpower' method still craving occasional cigarettes years after smoking what they hoped would be their last? And why do so many of them get hooked again?

BECAUSE SMOKING ISN'T A HABIT, IT'S NICOTINE ADDICTION

Once you understand the true nature of the trap, you will see clearly that attempts to cut down or to control the level that you smoke ingrains into your brain the idea that you cannot enjoy life or cope with stress without a cigarette.

Imagine the 'little monster' as an almost imperceptible itch. We've all been told that scratching an itch will only make it worse, and yet our instinctive response to an itch is to do just that.

With the 'little monster', the instinctive response is to light a cigarette. As soon as you do, you get some relief, but this relief will be only temporary and, because you've scratched it, the itch will get worse.

Can't get no satisfaction

It was once common for tobacco manufacturers to advertise their brands as 'satisfying' or as 'giving satisfaction'. It doesn't take a genius to deduce that it is not possible to satisfy a given situation without a previous state of dissatisfaction.

For example, we satisfy a sexual desire, a hunger or a thirst. But you won't satisfy a sexual desire by eating or a thirst by smoking a cigarette. The only aggravation that a cigarette appears to satisfy is the nicotine 'itch', although the relief is only temporary because nicotine is responsible for causing the itch in the first place. Non-smokers don't suffer from this particular aggravation.

As immunity to the relief sets in, the 'itch' becomes permanent and the natural tendency is to scratch it all the time: in other words, to chain-smoke.

So why don't we all quickly become chain-smokers?

Because you need very strong lungs to chain-smoke, believe me. Many smokers cannot physically cope with more than five to ten cigarettes a day. It also costs a lot of money, which many smokers simply cannot afford, and so they are forced to battle and fight their addiction every single day.

In this way every smoker who doesn't chain-smoke is suffering the frustration of not being able to scratch their itch as often as they want to. This is the torture that all casual smokers endure.

There are several reasons why many women are casual smokers nowadays and they all involve feelings of guilt, self-despising and the use of massive self-discipline. A common reason for limiting their intake is because they want to set an example to their children and grandchildren.

Every smoker who doesn't chain-smoke is suffering the frustration of not being able to scratch their itch as often as they want to

Take a closer look at the 'I can take it or leave it' smokers. Notice how restless they become when they haven't had a cigarette for a period, and how quickly they find an excuse to have a sneaky puff.

See the whole tug-of-war as it really is:

- on one side a permanent 'itch' with an accompanying desire to scratch it permanently
- on the other side powerful reasons for wishing that you didn't need to scratch it at all.

Cutting down or casual smoking – which amount to the same thing – cannot work, because scratching the 'itch' is the only pleasure any smoker ever gets from smoking.

'I can take it or leave it, but I'm dying for one right now.'

The more you scratch it, the more immune you become to the relief, which makes you want to chain-smoke. But the more you smoke, the greater is the destruction of your health, wealth, nerves, concentration and courage.

What a terrible trap drug addiction is: part of your brain wants to smoke more, and whenever you do the other part wants you to smoke less.

'People doubted that I would quit. After reading Easyway I stopped instantly. I proved not only myself wrong but others and felt so amazing. I went on to quit my job that I was stuck in for six years and started a new career. It literally changed my life. I cannot believe how easy it was.'
Tara M, Ireland

The more you smoke, the less you want to smoke. The less you smoke, the more you want to smoke.

Smokers can never win.

When you cut down, you discipline yourself not to relieve the 'itch' immediately. Just as the longer you wear tight shoes, the greater will be the sense of relief when you finally take them off, so the longer you suffer the 'itch', the greater will be the illusion of pleasure when you finally allow yourself to scratch it.

This enhancement of the illusion of pleasure actually has the effect of reducing your desire to stop.

The less you smoke, the more you want to smoke

This is why casual smokers are more hooked than heavy smokers.

'I've been thinking about nothing else all day.'

If you have suffered the misery of a 'willpower' method of trying to 'give up', it is difficult to imagine that the process of stopping smoking can be immediate, easy and enjoyable.

But would you get any feeling of relief from tight shoes unless you wore them? Would you miss that feeling of relief if you didn't wear them? Of course not.

Smoking is a strange pastime. When we are allowed to do it, we cannot understand what pleasure we get, and wish we didn't have to do it. Only when we aren't allowed to do it does it appear to be pleasurable.

Falling back in

Have you ever got to the stage where you have 'given up' long enough to feel so certain you've kicked it that you want to take a couple of puffs, just to prove the point? If you've done this, you'll know that not only does it taste bad but it does nothing for you whatsoever. However, it does convince you that you couldn't get hooked again. So a week or so later, you feel confident that you can have just one cigarette without getting hooked again. You've fallen into exactly the same trap that you fell into at the start.

Is it so difficult to believe that if no 'little monster' or nicotine 'itch' existed, and you didn't need to discipline yourself not to scratch it for a week, there would be no need or desire to relieve it?

And even if you did, there would be no feeling of relief?

What we are trying to achieve is a frame of mind such that you have no more need or desire to smoke a single cigarette than you have to inject yourself with heroin.

This is why cutting down cannot work. It not only keeps the 'little monster' alive, but actually increases the power of the 'big monster'.

One is enough

Some 'experts' will advise you that you only need to resist the temptation of smoking just one cigarette: the next one. And the great evil of this statement is that it is true. What they fail to tell you is that if you see that one cigarette as some sort of support or pleasure, you are going to have to spend the rest of your life resisting it!

Cutting down on nicotine means going through life suffering the double-aggravation of the 'itch' itself and not being allowed to scratch it when you want to. Such a situation demands permanent willpower and discipline.

This process intrinsically increases the desire to smoke and reduces the desire to stop. Even if you had the willpower to stand this situation for the rest of your life, do you really want to go through that misery?

Does dieting make food appear to be less precious? Of course not. Your whole life turns into an obsession with food. After each meal either you feel guilty because you didn't stick to your diet, or hungry and dissatisfied because you did.

It's not wise to assume that casual smokers are happy just because they keep telling you they are, or because we've been brainwashed into assuming that happy, casual smokers exist.

'Do as I say, not as I do.'

Many smokers will tell you how much they enjoy being smokers, but you try to find just one intelligent smoking parent who encourages their children to smoke. This goes for happy, casual smoking parents too.

Talk to these happy, casual smokers. Talk to them privately and you will find that many admit that they would rather be non-smokers. It doesn't take much probing to realize that the others are hiding behind a shield based on fear.

It's incredible that the human race survived hundreds of thousands of years without cancer. In 1900 only one in 50 UK citizens died from cancer. Today it's one in four. Why do we blame our parents or the incredible intelligence that designed us? If you were stupid enough to pour salt water over your car on a daily basis, would you blame the manufacturer for its being riddled with rust?

The smoker's 'itch' is a feeling of emptiness, insecurity and lack of courage and confidence.

If you are ever tempted to envy a casual smoker again, remember they spend the bulk of their lives suffering that empty, insecure feeling.

This also applies to the 'stoppers and starters': the 'I don't find "giving up" a problem, I can do it whenever I want to' type. It doesn't take a Miss Marple to deduce that smokers who can 'give up' whenever they want to just don't exist.

'I'm down to five a day, but I can't seem to stop completely.'

Lack of willpower?

In the next chapter we will explode the myth that smokers who have failed to stop are lacking in willpower. In particular, we will explode the myth that the reason there are more women smoking than men, and more young girls getting hooked than boys, is because women are in general weaker, less intelligent, more ruled by emotion than logic and less strong-willed than men.

Dr Tai Hing Lam (University of Hong Kong) says, 'Many older smokers believe they are too old to quit or to benefit from quitting.' The fact is, you're never too old to stop smoking; it will always make life better.

To start with, it's a contradiction in terms: if they have truly 'given up', they wouldn't have started again. Not once, let alone several times. And why would they want to 'give up'?

No smoker would 'give up' unless they didn't enjoy being a smoker. And when they do 'give up', why on earth do they start again?

The answer is obvious:

They don't enjoy being a smoker or a non-smoker.

Never forget that, although all smokers are different, they are all hooked on the same drug. It's not a case of one man's food is another man's poison; this particular drug is poisonous to all living creatures. To each and every one of them it is undiluted

DEVASTATION

Warning
Please don't envy the stoppers and starters. Like every other smoker, heavy, casual or otherwise, they actually get the worst of all worlds.

'Stoppers and starters? I stop and start at least 20 times a day.'

It is a common belief: once a smoker, always a smoker. In other words, no matter how many years you've 'given up', an ex-smoker will never feel the same as someone who never fell into the trap.

This is true for the vast majority of ex-smokers, because with a 'willpower' method you do believe that you have given up a genuine support or pleasure.

With Easyway you actually feel better than a non-smoker.

Many non-smokers actually suspect that *they* are missing out. After all, they too are subjected to the massive brainwashing. And why would any of us be tempted to try those first experimental cigarettes unless we suspected that there was some pleasure or support?

Their attitude tends to be, what you've never had you don't miss.

With Easyway you see quitting smoking as it really is: waking from a frightening nightmare.

CHAPTER 15

The truth about willpower

Most people – not only smokers – believe it takes willpower to stop smoking.

So powerful is this particular myth that the controllers of TV and radio advertising won't allow a stop smoking commercial to be broadcast unless it includes a statement to the effect that the aid will only work in conjunction with the smoker's own willpower.

It's not surprising that smokers who fail to stop feel that they are weak-willed. We have been subjected to massive brainwashing from birth to the effect that 'giving up' can be very difficult but with sufficient willpower you can succeed.

So when someone tries and fails to quit umpteen times when using willpower, what other explanation is there, other than that they are a weak-willed jellyfish?

It's not surprising that smokers who fail to stop feel that they are weak-willed

But how can this be the case for so many people who are patently strong-willed in other aspects of their life?

Because 'giving up' smoking has nothing to do with willpower. It is a conflict of wills.

Just open your mind and the facts clearly explode the myths.

Looking back

Look back at your schooldays, when some groups of girls experimented and others didn't. Which girls led the way? Was it the shy, retiring ones or the physically strong and dominant? Who were the role models who helped so many teenage girls fall into the trap? Wasn't it the Elle Macphersons, Joanna Lumleys, Kate Mosses? Do any of them strike you as being weak-willed?

Smokers don't smoke because they're unaware of the harm it does to their health. The real challenge is to remove the reasons that make them continue to smoke.

While we might be influenced by peer pressure, advertising and other brainwashing to fall into the trap and to remain in it, no one can force us either to smoke a cigarette or not to smoke one.

Make your own mind up

Every year the 'media' declares the second Wednesday in March 'National No Smoking Day'. This is the day every smoker is supposed to decide to 'give up'. Yet every smoker will tell you that it is the one day in the year they will do their utmost to resist such pressure. Just to reinforce the point, many will smoke more blatantly and twice as many cigarettes as usual.

The connection between smoking and lung cancer has been established for nearly half a century. Do they really believe it helps to tell smokers one day a year that smoking is harmful to health, when it's been written on every packet of cigarettes for the last umpteen years? Sadly, the so-called 'experts' don't understand the nature of the nicotine trap, let alone the solution.

It is equally obvious that when we try to 'give up', if we had no desire to light up, quitting would be a simple matter. But we've been brainwashed to believe that smoking gives us some pleasure and/or support.

Clinging to the illusion that we enjoy the ritual is a smokescreen we devise to justify a filthy, anti-social habit

It's like a see-saw. At one end are the 'goodies': the bad effect smoking has on our health and wealth. At the other end are the 'baddies': the belief that smoking supplies some sort of support or pleasure.

The see-saw moves and the weights of the 'goodies' and 'baddies' keeps changing. While we have no intention of quitting, we close our minds to the health and wealth aspects and they effectively have no weight. During these periods, if we have no need or desire to light up, the 'goodies' prevail, keeping the 'baddies' high and dry.

Sooner or later the 'little monster' starts to 'itch'. The weight of the 'baddies' increases and the balance is tipped. When we light a cigarette, the desire is satisfied and down come the 'goodies' again.

When we decide to 'give up', we open our minds to the 'goodies', substantially increasing their combined weight so that, even when the 'little monster' signals to the brain, 'I want or need a cigarette', the response is, 'I'm afraid you can't have one.'

Hold on – shouldn't these 'goodies' be the 'baddies'?

No! This is part of the confusion that the nicotine trap creates in our minds. The belief that smoking supplies some sort of support or pleasure makes you want to continue to smoke, so they are the real 'baddies'. The genuine destruction of your health and wealth are forces that make you want to 'give up', so in this context they are the 'goodies'.

Now the 'big monster' comes into play. A slight 'itch' isn't such a problem, provided you can scratch it. But an itch that you can't scratch? That can drive you crazy!

Even worse, the itch is easily accessible to you but you won't allow yourself to scratch it!

If you have an itch that part of your brain wants you to scratch, it would take an enormous feat of willpower to resist scratching it. But this doesn't mean that a strong-willed person will resist longer than a weak-willed person.

But an itch that you can't scratch? That can drive you crazy!

Regardless of the strength of their respective willpower, both people have a conflict of wills.

Before the association between smoking and lung cancer was made, most smokers were happy to put up with smoker's cough, asthma, bronchitis and general lethargy, regarding them as a small price to pay for their pleasure and crutch. But the risk of cancer added considerable weight to the 'goodies'. Were the people who stopped as a result really being sensible and strong-willed, or were they simply panicking and being cowardly?

Smokers who have failed to stop tend to be dominant, strong-willed people.

The cigarettes that make it difficult for us to 'give up' aren't the ones we claim to enjoy most but the ones we need, or the ones we cannot survive without; for example, when we have to concentrate or are under stress.

Dominant, strong-willed people tend to take on more responsibility and stress is part and parcel of their lives. Cigarettes go with their lifestyle.

Smokers who have failed to stop tend to be dominant, strong-willed people

Millions of smokers have deliberately switched brands or to roll-ups, cigars or pipes, in the hope that this will help them to 'give up', cut down or save money.

'There must be a better way of getting my nicotine fix.'

It isn't long before the new brand becomes their favourite and their previous favourite becomes offensive – further proof that taste or enjoyment has nothing to do with smoking.

It's just the nicotine we are after.

If you've tried herbal cigarettes, you'll know that no matter how long you persevere, you will never achieve even the illusion of pleasure by smoking them. Smoking herbal cigarettes is just like breathing bad fumes into your lungs. The reason that they'll never give you the illusion of enjoyment is that they contain no nicotine.

The reason that your favourite brand appears to taste better than other brands is because you have trained your lungs to become partially immune to that particular concoction of poisons. But have you noticed how smokers whose brand isn't available for some reason will smoke old rope rather than go without?

Cigarettes do absolutely nothing for you whatsoever. You must understand why this is so and accept it. That way, there's no feeling of deprivation. Remember, there's no such thing as an 'occasional cigarette'. See it as it really is: the whole filthy lifetime's chain..

Why does the identical cigarette out of the same packet appear to taste marvellous after a meal, but bad if it's the first cigarette after the New Year's party?

Because it's not the smoking of the cigarette itself that's important, but the time at which you scratch the 'itch'.

After a meal, you have already satisfied two aggravations: your hunger and thirst, so you feel relaxed. The cigarette after the evening meal tends to taste better than the one you smoke after breakfast or lunch, because work for the day is over and you feel entitled to unwind and relax.

It's no wonder that a cigarette after a meal out or at friends' seems particularly pleasant

If someone else is doing the cooking, you feel even better. No wonder that a cigarette after a meal out or at friends' seems particularly pleasant.

It's not so much that smokers enjoy a cigarette after a meal or that it tastes any better than it does at any other time. The point is that unless they are allowed to scratch the 'itch', they do not feel relaxed at all.

The whole question of willpower is irrelevant

If they are not allowed to smoke, they actually feel deprived and miserable. The difference between smoking and not smoking at such a time is the difference between paradise and purgatory.

That's why the cigarette after a meal or with a drink appears to taste better. In fact, the whole question of willpower is irrelevant.

Were the smokers who stopped when the lung cancer connection was established being sensible and strong-willed, or were they scared and weak-willed?

It makes no difference; either way, the scare increased the weight of the 'goodies'.

The problem is, the moment you try to 'give up', the combined weight of the 'goodies' tends to decrease. You are no longer risking awful diseases, burning your money or despising yourself for being a slave to nicotine.

'Stop? I don't know if I've got what it takes.'

All the powerful forces that made you want to 'give up' in the first place are rapidly disappearing. The facts don't actually change but your perception of them does.

Meanwhile, the weight of the 'baddies' is increasing, because when you 'give up', you believe that you have made a genuine sacrifice. You've had to resist scratching the 'itch' for a few days, all of which is making you feel deprived and miserable.

We all know in our rational minds that the combined weight of the 'goodies' (reasons for being a non-smoker) far exceeds the combined weight of the 'baddies' (the illusion of pleasure or support). But it takes just one weak, stupid, drunken or unguarded moment, when the 'baddies' appear to outweigh the 'goodies', for us to light up again.

Just one cigarette and you find yourself back in the trap.

Stop seeing smokers as jellyfish and a failure to stop as being due to lack of willpower. See it as it really is: a conflict of wills in which the strength of the combatants is continually varying.

Now look at the true position:

- That smoking not only doesn't confer any pleasure or crutch whatsoever, but actually destroys your nerves, confidence, courage and ability to concentrate and relax.
- That, far from relieving boredom and stress, smoking is a major cause of both.

Is it me?

It is obvious that smoking provides us with no physical advantages, nor does it provide pleasure or a crutch. The feeling of weakness, both physical and mental, that smokers experience is caused by the drug alone.

Supposing there was no conflict or confusion, that you could remove all the brainwashing, see smoking as it really is: Devastation – then you would have no need or desire to light a cigarette. If you have no need or desire to smoke, it doesn't take one bit of willpower not to. It is irrelevant whether you are weak-willed or otherwise.

Willpower is irrelevant.

One of the evils of all drug addiction is the ingraining into victims' minds that they have some intrinsic flaw in their physical and/or mental make-up and are dependent on the magic provided by the drug.

'I think
I deserve it,
don't you?'

Some smokers can see clearly that nicotine addiction simply creates an illusion of pleasure and/or crutch, are convinced and happy that they will never smoke again, but still feel that something is missing in their lives.

'It's my little reward.'

When you've truly believed that smoking offers a reward, you will feel that you've lost that reward, even though it is illusory.

If you can't kid yourself into believing that wearing tight shoes will solve the problem, what's the point of kidding yourself that Western society's No. 1 killer disease will solve the problem?

I say to ex-smokers who see a cigarette as a reward, 'No problem. You can get exactly the same effect by wearing tight shoes. Then whenever you need a little reward, just remove them for a few moments.'

They don't see this as a solution; in fact, they think I'm being facetious. But it does help them to see the true position.

If your lifestyle is boring and stressful, the only real solution is to change it. You'll probably find, as I did, that quitting smoking actually cured the boredom and the stress.

When you stop smoking, you don't need anything to take its place.

You were able to enjoy life and cope with stress before you became hooked – before you were tricked into believing that you needed phoney crutches or props.

You might well feel genuinely weak and insecure at the moment, even if you are a casual smoker. It is important when quitting smoking to realize that the feelings of weakness and insecurity are genuine.

It is even more important to realize that **these feelings are caused by smoking** – and that if you follow all the instructions, courage and confidence that you had forgotten you had will return in no time at all.

You were able to enjoy life and cope with stress before you became hooked

I know you will find this difficult to believe if you have ever gone through the torture of a 'willpower' attempt to 'give up'. I assure you that it is true.

CHAPTER 16

Which is the stronger sex?

In Western society, the percentage of women who smoke is catching up with that of men. More and more young women are falling into the trap. Why should this be so?

Women smokers' feelings of weakness and insecurity are compounded by the fact that they are subjected to a heinous form of brainwashing that is not applied to men.

This brainwashing would have us all believe that women are not only physically weaker than men, but are generally less intelligent, less logical, more emotional and less able to take responsibility.

But we have already established that the dominant and strong-willed representatives of both sexes tend to be the role models who assist the rest of us into the trap. We can't have it both ways.

Even today there is an assumption that men are generally stronger than women, both physically and mentally. It is a 'fact' that for generations we have been conditioned to believe.

The logical conclusion is that if smokers tend to be physically and mentally stronger than non-smokers, modern woman must be stronger than modern man. In truth she always has been!

'We all have our weaknesses, darling!'

If a friend tells you that she 'must eat', you know she has a genuine need for food and won't be happy until she has satisfied her hunger. You understand and accept the distinction between someone needing food and simply fancying a bite.

Many non-smokers find it difficult to understand why a smoker would even want a cigarette, let alone need one. But a non-smoker who is involved with a heavy smoker can see clearly that it is not a want but a need.

The non-smoker can't understand why this should be so, but is in no doubt that the smoker is dependent and enslaved.

The 'experts' spend many hours speculating why youngsters fall into the trap. Like every other aspect of nicotine addiction, they would learn so much more by researching the opposite: why other youngsters don't fall into it.

My mother watched my father die from lung cancer. How it must have pained her to watch me become a smoker. She did, however, know instinctively the sway that my wife held over me. She said to Joyce, 'Why don't you threaten to leave him if he doesn't give up?'

Joyce replied, 'Because he can't give up and would let me leave.'

Joyce, also a non-smoker, could no more understand the stupidity than could my mother, but she could see that I wasn't smoking because I wanted to, but because I believed that I couldn't enjoy or cope with life without it.

The distinction between 'wanting' and 'needing' a cigarette is very important to smokers themselves. They will willingly admit to needing food or, providing they are not alcoholic, a drink. But they will never admit to needing a cigarette.

Smokers will go to great lengths to try and prove to their friends, and to themselves, that they are in control and don't 'need' a cigarette. It doesn't seem to occur to them that they are simply proving the exact opposite.

I wasn't smoking because I wanted to, but because I believed that I couldn't enjoy or cope with life without it

The sociable cigarettes, like the one after a meal, appear to be the most pleasurable, but we can survive without that illusion. It's when we are under stress that we really 'need' a cigarette.

It's when we are under stress that we really 'need' a cigarette

Women generally have more roles to juggle in their lives than men.

Women's liberation has done much to help improve the rights and status of women in Western society. Ironically, some of the gains have served only to increase the stress in a woman's life.

To be treated equally in professions that were once regarded as the preserve of men, a woman has to be ten times as good as her male counterpart.

Most career women not only have the stress of the career itself to cope with, but also the traditional stresses of pregnancy, childbirth and parenting – and the latter sometimes applies to her husband as well!

'I'm exercising my equal right to self-destruction.'

A word of warning

You might well conclude from what I've been saying that it is more difficult for women to stop smoking, or even that you would be wise to continue to smoke. Not so. All I am saying is that, whether it's fair or not, women tend to have more stress in their lives than men. That being so, they are more likely to fall into the smoking trap. But you don't need to worry about this any more. You're about to escape!

Get it clearly into your mind: smoking doesn't relieve stress, it causes it. Indeed, for most smokers nicotine addiction is not only the major cause of their stress, but it's what causes so many other aspects of their lives to appear stressful too.

I'm not just referring to the effect that the cumulative poisoning and financial cost has on your physical and mental health, energy and self-respect, although all of these factors increase the stress in our lives. I'm also referring to the anxious, empty, insecure feeling that nicotine creates.

Get it clear: smoking doesn't relieve stress, it causes it

The effect on smokers is to transform trivial, everyday setbacks, which non-smokers take in their stride, into great traumas.

I used to think that the only reason I became a chain-smoker was because of the stress created by the fact that I hated my job. The true reason was my addiction to nicotine, which caused me to have the stress in the first place.

Assume for a moment that cigarettes did relieve stress. You'd expect smokers to be relatively calm and laid-back compared to non-smokers. But isn't it the smokers who seem to be uptight and restless, particularly when they aren't allowed to smoke?

Haven't you found yourself yelling at the kids to go to sleep so you can 'safely' sneak outside for a cigarette? Isn't it the smokers who always need something to do with their hands or something to calm their nerves?

If cigarettes do calm their nerves, why do smokers remain so nervous?

Haven't you found yourself yelling at the kids to go to sleep so you can 'safely' sneak outside for a cigarette?

CHAPTER 17

Smoking during pregnancy

Your life will be less stressful once you have stopped smoking. It's vital that you understand this, especially if you happen to be facing the single most stressful time in a woman's life: pregnancy.

This is without doubt one of the big taboos. There is no comparable situation in which smokers are made to feel so bad about themselves.

Interesting to note, most smokers who are pregnant agree wholeheartedly with their accusers and will contribute to the scorn heaped upon them.

The many letters I receive from smoking mothers are full of self-blame and self-loathing. The women condemn themselves for setting a bad example to their children and for running the risk of leaving them motherless.

Those who swore that they would 'give up' if ever they became pregnant feel even worse about themselves.

'Have one of mine, darling. You're smoking for two now.'

This extract from a letter from Jean is an extreme example:

'One little cigarette shouldn't do too much harm.'

'It's ironic that during the first four years of our marriage we went to enormous lengths to avoid me getting pregnant. We are both fit and healthy (in spite of my smoking) and didn't dream that there would be any problems when the time was right. I won't bore you with the horrors of the tests we both went through, but after eight years of trying we both reached the stage of believing it would never happen and were seriously considering adoption.

'Then the miracle happened. I won't attempt to explain the exhilaration. I couldn't wait for my husband to get home from work to share the good news.

'I'd been in the habit of carefully rationing out a packet of cigarettes a day, always leaving at least five for the morning. I went to light up and found I was down to my last two. It was only about five o'clock and I realized that I'd been chain-smoking since I'd got home.

'After eight years of trying we both reached the stage of believing it would never happen'

'Pregnancy's a very stressful time, you know! I need something to help me through it.'

'In the circumstances this was no great surprise to me but the great shock was that it reminded me that I'd promised Eric and myself that I would give up if I was lucky enough to get pregnant.

'In fact, one of the reasons that I'd looked forward to conceiving was to give up smoking! Far from looking forward to it, suddenly all my exhilaration was replaced by sheer panic.

'I didn't tell Eric. Although he's never been a smoker, he has always been considerate and never nagged me to give up, even though I know he hates smoking.

'I'm now in my fifth month, it's beginning to show and I still haven't told him. At first I made the excuse that it was too early and I didn't want to raise his hopes, only to have them dashed. I now know that the true reason I haven't told him is that I cannot face the thought of attempting to stop.

The 'power' of nicotine addiction is in the panic feeling of believing that you cannot enjoy life or cope with life without a cigarette. That panic feeling is real. But once you understand that each cigarette, far from relieving the panic feeling, is actually the cause of it, that power not only ceases to exert any control over you, but actually becomes the most effective force to *prevent* you from craving another cigarette.

'How can I expect him to understand, especially after all the trouble we went through? I feel so depressed and miserable. I couldn't feel worse if I had been unfaithful to him – and that's how I do feel: that I've been unfaithful to him.

'It's not as if I don't believe that smoking affects an unborn baby's health. I do. I know what it's doing to me. Even that doesn't make me stop. I'm sure I'm a hopeless case and don't suppose you can help me.'

Some people think they are beyond help. We are delighted to prove them wrong and help them walk to freedom

Getting the point

I didn't advise Jean to attempt to 'give up'. Instead I suggested that she should come along to the clinic with her husband. Jean was well aware of the effect nicotine has. She thought, 'The power this evil holds over me is so great that I'll never be able to escape it, let alone find quitting easy.' During our session, she grasped the important point that cigarettes weren't relieving her panic, they were causing it.

Both Jean and her husband Eric were intelligent people. At the end of the session, he put his arms around her and said, 'I understand now. Don't even try to stop unless you want to.' Bear in mind that, at this stage, he still didn't know that she was pregnant. She replied, 'I've already smoked my last cigarette.' Then she told him about the baby.

Jean's was an extreme case, but only in degree; in substance it is all too common.

Society makes it so easy for young girls to get hooked; they are almost forced into the trap. Then, when they become pregnant and enter probably the most stressful period in their lives to date, we subject them to massive pressure designed to shame them into 'giving up'.

Society makes it easy for young girls to get hooked; they are almost forced into the trap

Pregnancy has become a catalogue of tests, options, decisions, joy, excitement and fear. If they fail the quitting smoking test at this time, we treat them with contempt and berate them for their 'weakness'.

This attitude is understandable from the medical profession, even though it's not particularly helpful to either the mother or the unborn child. But non-smokers, ex-smokers, relatives and strangers seem to feel justified and obliged to add their bit of abuse.

A little empathy here!

This inability to empathize is typical of human nature, unfortunately. When you've got a bad cold and are feeling very miserable with it, how many times has someone commented irritably, 'What are you making such a fuss about? You've only got a cold!'

This leaves them with a guilty conscience for the rest of their lives

Some girls are lucky and simply lose the desire to smoke during their pregnancy. Others make a conscious decision to stop, but sadly fail. Even if the baby is born healthy, this leaves them with a guilty conscience for the rest of their lives. It's hard to imagine what miseries they suffer if the baby is born with some disability.

Some women succeed in stopping during their pregnancy. Then, after nine months of discomfort, fear, expectation and excitement, comes the most stressful period of their lives: the fear, pain, mental and physical exhaustion of the labour, culminating in the miracle of the birth.

If all is well with both mother and child, the fear has gone, the pain and exhaustion are momentarily forgotten, the mother is instantaneously lifted from the lowest of lows to the highest of highs. These are the two extremes in a smoker's life, when the brain is triggered to shout,

I NEED A CIGARETTE!

More women stop smoking during pregnancy than at any other time, but 25 per cent begin again within a year of giving birth. If the woman's partner smokes, she is less likely to quit.

Some women who stopped smoking for the major part of the pregnancy tell me that they lit up before the cord was cut. Some resist the immediate impulse and are then caught out later on. Regrettably, very few stop permanently because of pregnancy. Like all reasons for stopping, once the reason no longer applies, neither does the desire not to smoke.

Many pregnant girls either refuse to believe the adverse effects that smoking has on their unborn child, or try to justify themselves by saying, 'I think it would do the baby more harm than good if I attempted to stop at this stage.' Some even claim that their doctor actually forbade them to stop for this reason.

I could write a separate book about the statements doctors have purportedly made about smoking.

One woman who found she lost the desire to smoke during her first pregnancy, but got hooked again immediately after, told me she deliberately got pregnant again, not because she wanted another child, but to help her to stop smoking! Initially it struck me as somewhat bizarre, but the more I thought about it the more sense it made. The problem was it didn't work.

Think of baby
The last thing a pregnant woman wants to read about is the damage she is causing her baby by smoking. She already knows, and it didn't make her stop.

With the best of intentions, many doctors advise pregnant mothers to try to cut down if they cannot stop completely. The advice sounds logical but it is the worst of the three choices that the mother has.

Not only does she suffer the extra stress of this self-imposed restriction for the whole nine months, she also suffers guilt whenever she exceeds the intake limit on a bad day.

The really damaging aspect is that it ingrains into the mother's mind the illusion of just how precious each cigarette is.

After the birth the mother is in the same position as a dieter who can no longer sustain the feeling of deprivation. The dieter goes on a binge; the smoker goes on an orgy of smoking.

The more anxious, uptight and insecure other people make a pregnant woman feel, the greater is her need for the illusory crutch.

The dieter goes on a binge;
the smoker goes on an orgy of smoking

She's lost control

Apart from the pregnancy itself and the vilification that goes with it, pregnant smokers are often hit by an additional shock at this time. Most smoking youngsters are convinced that they are in control and could stop if ever the need arose. Pregnancy is often the event that makes them realize they are just one among millions, another nicotine 'junkie'!

There is one aspect of the effect smoking has on a baby's health that I do feel bound to mention. I have read that babies whose mothers are addicted to heroin will suffer withdrawal symptoms themselves. It follows that the same principle should apply to nicotine addiction.

When a smoker feels the discomfort of withdrawal from nicotine, they immediately relate it to cigarettes. In other words, they have some idea what's happening to them.

Imagine how horrible it must be for a baby to feel the pangs of nicotine withdrawal

Imagine how horrible it must be for a baby to feel the pangs of nicotine withdrawal and have absolutely no idea what's causing it.

Babies are programmed to cry when they are hungry. A baby that is suffering the physical withdrawal effects from nicotine will feel permanently hungry and will keep crying.

Feeding it won't satisfy that feeling. The tired and confused mother will tend to overfeed it and, by doing so, will exacerbate the problem.

Let's get back to the point.

Whether you are pregnant or otherwise, I want you to stop smoking for the purely selfish reason that you will enjoy life so much more as a happy non-smoker.

If you have a genuine problem and you are able to do something about it, do it! If there is absolutely nothing that you can do about it, accept the fact. Worrying about it won't help.

If you are a smoker, you do have a serious and genuine problem. Fortunately there is a simple and easy solution:

STOP SMOKING!

CHAPTER 18

The myth that smoking helps to reduce weight

I've lost count of the number of women who have told me that they deliberately took up smoking to lose weight. In fact, smoking doesn't help you to lose weight. Like all the other illusions, it actually has the opposite effect.

Even if smoking did help to reduce weight, I don't believe any smoker deliberately chose to become a smoker for the rest of their life for that, or any other reason. It is very important that you realize this.

What would you think if I said, 'Not a single person, past or present, has decided to make a regular practice of placing their hand in boiling water in order to get the relief of removing it.' You might think this is so obvious as to be worthless as an argument.

The real difference between the two is that with smoking we are fooled into believing that it gives us some genuine pleasure or crutch.

> If we could see smoking as it really is – as utterly lacking in beneficial effects as sticking your hand in boiling water – no one would choose to get hooked.

Other smokers are an important influence on getting us hooked, and in making us feel that we are missing out when we have managed to stop.

- No smoker smokes because they choose to or want to.
- They are receiving no benefits from smoking.
- All smokers wish they had never started.

Even if we believe in the illusory benefits of smoking, we have no logical reason for becoming hooked deliberately.

What are these illusory benefits?

That smoking is pleasurable?

The first cigarette tells us it's a pleasure we could well do without. We also know that it is unhealthy, filthy and disgusting.

That it helps us to concentrate and to relax, and to relieve stress and boredom?

Before we become smokers, we are perfectly able to concentrate

Before we become smokers we are perfectly capable of concentrating, relaxing and even coping with boredom and stress without breathing filthy fumes into our lungs. So why would we logically risk the downside for benefits that we don't actually need?

The only logical reason for deliberately becoming hooked on smoking would be to commit suicide. But if you genuinely wished to shorten your life, it is hard to imagine a more prolonged, painful, expensive, excruciating and ineffective method of achieving that goal.

There is no logical reason whatsoever to choose to smoke.

'One cigarette leads to another… there's no getting around it.'

You might argue that an overweight adolescent, anxious to attract a partner, might believe that smoking will help her to lose weight. The fact is she's been brainwashed into thinking it will help her lose weight, even if the truth is it doesn't. We all started smoking for a variety of foolish reasons, but we didn't expect to spend the rest of our lives carrying on smoking, never being allowed to stop.

The advertising of cigarettes has changed radically, and the most powerful persuaders of the 'sexiness' or 'coolness' of smoking are not being peddled openly by the tobacco companies themselves. When youngsters see the likes of Kate Moss and other slim, attractive fashion/media stars puffing away, they want to buy into that image. What they are being sucked in by is **free advertising** for Big Tobacco and its cynical opportunism.

The issue of body image projected by the media and the corresponding rise in eating disorders became such a hot issue in the 1990s that government intervention was sought to prevent the overuse of emaciated models, both male and female, in an attempt to curb the trend.

It has long been the practice of tobacco companies to feature beautiful people in their advertisements to glamourize their toxic products.

Sadly, far too many celebrities still allow themselves to be photographed smoking in public.

Smokers are the greatest salespeople the tobacco companies could wish for. They keep telling each other how lost they'd be without cigarettes and how hard it is to stop.

'So glad I finally gave it a chance, I have been cigarette free for 12 months today. My daughter also read the book and has been free for 3 months! I tell everyone I know about it and I buy it for friends' birthdays. I can't recommend it highly enough.'
Caroline M, Australia

Surely no one would actually resort to deliberately getting hooked on the No. 1 killer in Western society and spending a fortune during their lifetime just to lose weight, unless they had tried and failed by using more logical or conventional methods.

Perhaps they didn't believe they would get hooked and didn't work out what it would cost them financially.

Next time you are out, I'd like you to play a detection game. It's called spot the overweight smoker. I guarantee you'll find it a real eye-opener. They're everywhere.

It's true. A subtlety of the trap is that many teenagers dabble because they believe they won't get hooked.

But if you lack the self-discipline to control your food consumption, what makes you think you can resist nicotine addiction? After all, we all know how powerful nicotine is.

A subtlety of the trap is that many teenagers believe they won't get hooked

Would anyone deliberately take up smoking for any reason, let alone one as obtuse as losing weight, if they knew that their first cigarette would cost them a fortune and trap them for life? In fact, if most of us had had to pay for our first cigarettes, we wouldn't have fallen into the trap.

Avoiding the cost

Even when we are trying to 'give up', we bend the truth. We speak of saving so much money a week, when what we are actually doing is no longer squandering so much. Why we are so vague is because we don't wish to remind ourselves that we have a £100,000/$160,000-a-lifetime burden hanging round our necks.

All smokers lie.

They don't mean to. It's simply a fact about all addiction. Addicts lie to themselves and to others too.

If they can find some seemingly logical explanation – such as 'I only took it up to lose weight' – they will cling to it.

The fact that you won't find a single intelligent smoker in Western society who doesn't openly advise their children not to smoke is proof positive that no smoker continues to smoke because they choose to. Every smoker instinctively knows that they have fallen into a trap.

Many smokers will admit that they would dearly love to be free. Others won't, and in order to save face they will bend the truth.

Never forget that every smoker would love nothing better than to leave the sinking ship.

Why do we believe that smoking helps to reduce weight? Because there is plenty of evidence that it does. Whenever one of our friends brags that she hasn't smoked for six months, we congratulate her for looking so much healthier because of it. Secretly, though, aren't we thinking, 'That new wardrobe must have cost her a fortune!'?

Immortal words

If your parents smoked, or an auntie or cousin, you will have heard the immortal words, 'I tried to give up but put on so much weight I started again.' When you yourself try to escape from the trap, this is dredged out of your consciousness as one of those 'facts' about smoking.

It's true that most smokers who manage to stop using a 'willpower' method do put on weight.

The weight gain is also permanent for many ex-smokers. The obvious conclusion is that smoking must help to reduce weight. As with all other aspects of smoking, once you fully understand the nature of the trap, the opposite proves to be the case.

'Stop smoking? You're telling me I won't balloon up in size?!!'

If you've had a go at playing Spot the Overweight Smoker, you will have noticed that, in fact, most heavy smokers are also overweight.

A smoker is more likely to light a cigarette than eat. The evening meal then tends to take a more significant place in the smoker's mind – by this time of the day the body is genuinely hungry.

When we've eaten this evening meal, we can be left with an empty feeling, even though what we've had was substantial. Naturally we believe that our hunger hasn't been satisfied, particularly as we've eaten nothing all day.

What's really happened is that during the day your body was demanding food but your brain interpreted the feeling as, 'I want a cigarette'. So you smoked instead of eating. In the evening your body was actually craving nicotine, but your brain interpreted it as, 'You are hungry, eat more food.' Because they don't understand this, many smokers keep on eating, but don't manage to reach a state of satisfaction, because their body continues to crave nicotine.

> Food won't satisfy a craving for nicotine any more successfully than nicotine will satisfy a hunger for food.

Even though they didn't eat all day, they still put on weight.

So why do smokers put on weight when they try to 'give up'?

Because the 'little monster' does not die immediately and continues to crave nicotine for a short period.

The natural tendency is to substitute food.

Lots of it.

We have now reached the most difficult part of the process: the stage at which, I believe, the smokers who fail when using Easyway founder. It is absolutely essential that you fully understand the point I am making in the next few paragraphs.

This is an extract from a letter sent to me by Barbara:

Dear Allen,

I know several people who have stopped smoking after reading your book. I agree it is a wonderful book and understand and agree with everything you say. I've read it several times, but unfortunately it doesn't work for me.

I've tried several times but the longest I managed was three weeks. I'm a farmer's wife and we have four sons who all work on the farm. It is a very stressful life with long hours. Whenever I try to give up I can't stop thinking about smoking. I get very tearful and depressed...

Before I can address the points raised in Barbara's letter, I need to give you some information that I've been keeping from you. I told you that there were only five instructions. This is true. But these were just instructions to follow while you were reading the book.

There is another set of instructions, designed to keep you in a happy frame of mind for the rest of your life. Like choosing the right direction in a maze, each of these instructions is important. One of them is:

Forget even trying to stop thinking about smoking once you have stopped.

When we try to 'give up' using a 'willpower' method, we feel miserable because we are no longer allowed to smoke, but our mind is obsessed with the thought of smoking and so we try to discipline ourselves not to think about it.

But it's impossible to not think about something.

Stubbing out the 'little monster'

From the minute you cut off the supply of nicotine, the 'little monster' begins to die. In its death throes it will try to entice you to feed it. Think of it as a parasite. Create a mental image of it and enjoy starving it to death.

Barbara says, 'I can't stop thinking about smoking.' But why should she? Quitting smoking is probably the most beneficial decision you will ever make. How could you possibly not think about it?

Even if you tried not to think about smoking, for a few days the 'little monster' would be reminding you that he hasn't been fed. You'd have well-wishers enquiring about your progress. You might even have smoking friends deliberately breathing cigarette smoke into your face and trying to convince you, and themselves, that you are missing out.

No wonder Barbara found it impossible not to think about smoking.

Why compound the misery?

Ask yourself why you would want to <u>not</u> think about smoking? There's nothing bad happening; on the contrary, something marvellous is happening After so many years of freedom, the subject of no longer smoking takes up about 90 per cent of my waking and sleeping life.
Thinking about cigarettes or smoking isn't a problem – as long as you are thinking the right things. If you feel miserable and deprived, of course you'll hate thinking about it. But if you are happy to be free, you can think about it all day and it will bring you nothing but joy!

> 'I want to say how happy I am, after almost 38 years, to be smoke-free for over six weeks. I'm confident that this time there is no turning back. Yippee! I'm a non-smoker!'
> *Deb K, USA*

Barbara says, 'Whenever I try to give up, I can't stop thinking about smoking.' Obviously she still believes that she has made a sacrifice.

So when she thinks about smoking she does so in a negative, miserable frame of mind.

Clearly Barbara hasn't understood everything. The key is not whether or not you are thinking about smoking, but what you are thinking.

The key is not whether or not you are thinking about smoking, but what you are thinking

If you are thinking, 'When will I stop thinking about it?' or 'When will I stop feeling miserable and deprived?' you are simply ensuring that the answer to both questions is, 'Never!'

However, if you are thinking, 'Isn't it great! I'm already free!' you will be!

Is it really as simple as that? Whenever you think about smoking, just think, 'Isn't it great! I'm already free!'

No, it isn't.

It's no use trying to kid yourself and hoping that if you repeat it often enough it will eventually come true.

You continue to smoke for the sole reason that whenever you have previously tried to stop you found you couldn't concentrate, answer the phone, enjoy meals or cope with stress.

You didn't understand why this was so; you just knew that it was so. There was no way you could kid yourself that being deprived of the 'crutch' was great or that you were free.

Once you understand that...
- the nicotine trap is a clever confidence trick
- you didn't smoke because of some flaw or weakness
- nicotine, far from helping concentration or relaxation, was actually the cause of your inability to concentrate or relax

...then you'll find the situation turned on its head.

'Boy, am I glad that cigarette's gone. Now I can concentrate on the next one.'

There will be no way that you can kid yourself that you need to smoke.

Smokers who 'give up' using a 'willpower' method put on weight

Smokers who 'give up' using a 'willpower' method put on weight because, for the few days that the 'little monster' continues to create the empty, insecure feeling, they substitute food for nicotine.

Food not only becomes their answer to scratching the 'itch', it also becomes their 'reward'.

They are aware that chewing gum and sucking boiled sweets will make them put on weight, but they see it as a temporary measure and fully intend to stop doing it once they've kicked the 'habit'.

In no time at all, the ex-smoker is overweight, completely sick of sucking sweets and desperate for a cigarette. A valid excuse for having one has thus been created.

'I was not only killing myself being overweight but spending a fortune on new clothes. I thought I might just as well kill myself by smoking!'

The problem is that the sweet doesn't satisfy the craving for nicotine, and so you find yourself wanting another sweet and then another. Far from breaking the habit of a little reward, the sweets are actually perpetuating it.

You might know smokers who are very slim and have the shape of a supermodel. But, as Anita Roddick, the late founder of the Body Shop chain, pointed out, there are only seven supermodels in the world; the rest of us are normal.

Be clear about this: these ex-smokers don't put on weight because they stopped smoking, but because they fell into the trap in the first place.

Try to imagine the 'little monster' as a live tapeworm inside your body, which feeds on nicotine. How long do you have to starve it before it dies?

Most substitutes cause you to be overweight and miserable, and also actually make it harder for you to stop.

'Thank you so much for giving me the tools to save my life. I only hope I stopped in time. I am on my fifth day of NO SMOKING and I am thrilled! NO crabbiness, NO withdrawals, NO overeating. I want to run a marathon, so this was the first step to the rest of my life.'

Tiffany G, USA

Weight Gain?

There is no need to gain weight, even for a short period, when you use Easyway. Why? Because as long as you understand the method, there is no feeling of deprivation and therefore no need to substitute with food (or anything else for that matter).

There definitely isn't any chemical/biological reason why you should gain weight. Although smoking does speed up your metabolism, it does so marginally and not enough to have any serious impact on our weight. If you've ever worked out on an exercise bike, just remember how long and hard you have to peddle to burn off a couple of hundred calories! There really isn't some kind of special calorie/fat-burning going on as a result of smoking.

The only reason someone might gain weight when they stop smoking is as a result of eating more (or eating the wrong things). There are only a few causes of this and you are going to avoid all of them, so don't worry. First things first – it isn't because smoking is an appetite suppressant; it isn't particularly effective as that. As you now know, it's just a case of your brain mixing up hunger with nicotine withdrawal. Remember, in the past it's been you, and you alone, who has controlled what you've eaten – don't make the mistake of giving cigarettes the credit for that!

The most common reason for weight gain is substitution. If you are finding it hard not to smoke, you might be tempted to eat instead. Even if apparently innocent foods are eaten in this situation (vegetables or fruit), the results can still be negative. Any feeling of deprivation is made greater by substitution, which reinforces the feeling that something is missing, and endless misery results. But you won't feel deprived when you use Easyway, so you won't feel inclined to substitute. All you need to do is make sure you don't substitute as a matter of course (it's amazing how many people plan in advance to substitute, even before there is any apparent 'need'). Don't do it!

Another avoidable cause of weight gain can be what I call 'The Lap of Honour'. This is where someone has no desire to smoke – they are finding it easy – but also uses stopping smoking as an excuse to treat themselves to all sorts of things they wouldn't normally have. The attitude is very much 'Woo-hoo, I have done so well by not smoking, I should reward myself by having that biscuit, that cake, that pastry, that dessert, that chocolate bar' etc., etc. It is easy to imagine how this thought process and frame of mind can lead to over-eating (and over-eating the wrong kinds of foods). Actually worse than that, it can quickly create and then perpetuate a feeling of deprivation that was never there in the first place, creating a substitution issue all of its own. If you ever find yourself doing this, stay cool. Quickly put 'the brakes' on your lap of honour and start making the same decisions about what you eat as you've made all your life. It's time to move on and just rejoice at being a happy non-smoker. You will find this process easy.

The other issue may be that you have experienced peaks

and troughs in your weight throughout your lifetime with your weight going up and down regularly. In such cases, we often find ourselves wanting to blame a period of increased weight on something like having stopped smoking rather than just realizing that it's actually part of the normal pattern of our life. If this sounds like it applies to you, be sure to resume whatever regime it was that you enjoyed in the past. What better way to kick-start a healthier way of living than by stopping smoking?

The only other cause of over-eating (which again is easily avoidable) can be attributed to the renewal of your taste buds. Very quickly after you stop smoking, they return to normal and you may find that foods taste better than before. This is especially true of healthy foods such as fresh fruit and vegetables, so enjoy savouring these new tastes while being wary of less healthy ones. Make no mistake, enjoy the food you are used to, but be a little careful about eating more than normal because of your newly returned sense of taste.

You'll soon be taking your new found taste buds for granted and will no longer notice your heightened sense of taste. How long after wearing a smashing new coat is it before it becomes 'just your coat' rather than anything out of the ordinary?

Have no fear of weight gain. You're going to be a happy non-smoker and will suffer none of the disadvantages of the willpower methods.

You realize that you can enjoy life and cope without nicotine

Suddenly you realize that not only have you not smoked during this time, but the thought hasn't even occurred to you.

You realize that you can enjoy life and cope without being dependent on nicotine. You feel completely free!

This is a very pleasant feeling for any smoker, no matter what method of trying to stop they are using. It also happens to be a dangerous moment, one that has destroyed many otherwise successful attempts to stop.

Because you feel free, you might feel a compulsion to light a cigarette just to prove the fact. And it does just that! After three weeks of abstinence the cigarette tastes weird and foul. You get no feeling of pleasure or that nicotine is a crutch and are left wondering how you could have harboured those illusions.

But oh dear, you've put nicotine into your system again, and the moment it starts to leave, you've created a new 'little monster'.

Misleading myth
Smokers have been led to believe that cigarettes help overcome stress. But cigarettes only make stress worse, adding the itch to smoke to other irritations.

'We've got so much in common, even our cigarette brand.'

You probably won't scratch the 'itch' immediately, but a few days or weeks later, when you might be tempted again, you remember that you smoked one two weeks ago and didn't get hooked, so where's the harm?

You've landed in the same trap that you were in the first time round, and before you know it you're smoking as heavily as you did before.

Before you know it you're smoking as heavily as you did before

It is crucially important not to confuse the three-week period with the extended craving endured by smokers who try to 'give up' using a 'willpower' method. These smokers are not even aware of the 'little monster'.

Long after it has died, whenever they suffer an empty, insecure feeling, whether it be caused by a hunger for food, normal stress or anxiety, joy, or whatever, their brains will still be saying, 'That means you want a cigarette – you still haven't kicked it!'

> Now we have reached the nub of the most important and crucial difference between Easyway and 'willpower' methods.

Remember, the actual physical sensation of withdrawal is so slight that we are not even aware of its existence. It's just that empty feeling that has accompanied you throughout your smoking life without you being aware of it.

And it gets no worse when you stop.

The body cannot crave nicotine any more than it can crave food. All the body can do is send a signal to the brain, such as 'I'm hungry, I need to eat' or 'I want or need a cigarette'.

Be aware that, particularly during the first few days while the 'little monster' still lives, you might have the feeling of, 'I want or need a cigarette.'

> ***The body cannot crave nicotine any more than it can crave food***

With a 'willpower' method, the ex-smoker rationalizes the many powerful reasons why being a smoker is stupid. Yet, sometimes within just a few minutes of deciding you will never smoke another cigarette, part of the brain is saying, 'I want or need a cigarette.'

This is very confusing. We don't understand that it is just the death throes of the 'little monster'.

We assume that we want or need a cigarette because they provide us with some pleasure or crutch, or because we haven't yet broken the habit. The reason doesn't really matter. The fact is we want a cigarette but won't allow ourselves to have one. This makes us feel deprived and miserable.

Wanting a cigarette makes us feel deprived and miserable

Meanwhile, the 'little monster' hasn't been partially satisfied, and so the desire or need is gradually increasing. This makes you feel more deprived and miserable, which in turn creates distress.

When do you most feel the need for a cigarette? When you are under stress.

The greater the stress, the greater the need. The longer that need cannot be satisfied, the greater the stress. No wonder smokers 'giving up' with 'willpower' methods get so uptight and find it so difficult.

'If I'm honest, cigarettes only add stress to my life.'

With Easyway, when you have the feeling of, 'I want or need a cigarette', you understand that it is just the death throes of the 'little monster'. You know the feeling is a cruel confidence trick, brought on by the previous cigarette.

Instead of craving a cigarette and feeling deprived and miserable because you can't have one, your attitude is the complete opposite. You are reminded that smoking gives you neither pleasure nor a crutch, so no way are you going to be conned into breathing any more of this poison into your lungs. Your mindset is:

'Isn't it marvellous? I'm free!'

Instead of craving a cigarette and feeling deprived and miserable because you can't have one, your attitude is the complete opposite

Any changes in life, even changes for the better, take time to adjust to.

Have you noticed how, when you buy a new car, the switch that operates the windscreen wipers is always where the one to activate the indicators or horn was on your old car? For a few days, whenever you want to indicate, you hit the wipers or horn instead.

When you're getting used to a new car and you hit the windscreen wipers instead of the indicator, do you get all uptight and insist on deliberately repeating the act? No, you just accept that it takes time to adjust.

So accept that in the early days of stopping smoking your brain will probably shout, 'I want or need a cigarette!'

Accept that your brain will probably shout, 'I want or need a cigarette'

Realize that you are at liberty to make a choice. You can say to yourself, 'I'd love a cigarette now. How long will the craving last? Will I ever be free?' Or you can say to yourself, 'I understand this. It's simply the death throes of the "little monster". Isn't it marvellous? I'm already free!'

> Remember that any minor inconveniences you go through when quitting are caused because you fell into the trap in the first place. They are not caused because you're trying to stop.

And you will be.

But how will you know that you are not kidding yourself, that you really are free?

It's simple: you can't kid yourself that you are not dependent upon nicotine.

Nobody is ever dependent upon nicotine, not even smokers. They were simply fooled into believing that they were. With the 'willpower' method, smokers put out what they hope will be their last cigarette and then spend the next few days saying, 'I'd love a cigarette, but I mustn't have one!' Some of them spend the rest of their lives saying it.

Pause for a moment.

Just think of the stupidity of that situation. To say, 'I want to be a non-smoker,' then spend the rest of your life periodically saying, 'I'd love a cigarette.'

Nobody is ever dependent upon nicotine, not even smokers

Can you think of a worse case of muddled thinking?

What's the real difference between a smoker and a non-smoker?

Non-smokers have no need or desire to smoke.

Regardless of the method they are using, what are smokers really trying to achieve when they attempt to stop? Is it to go through life craving a cigarette at odd times and feeling miserable because they won't allow themselves to have one? Of course not!

When a smoker tries to 'give up', they cling to the forlorn hope that if they can abstain for long enough, they will wake up one morning and suddenly think, 'Isn't it great! I'm free! I'm a non-smoker!' The one thing you can be certain of is that they won't.

> 'I found your book and your method inspirational – I think the philosophy is brilliant and I think everyone should just read it even if they don't have a problem smoking. I have passed the book to several friends and they have got the rules too – fabulous! Thank you.'
>
> *Anne W, UK*

You don't need to wait to become a non-smoker.

Remove all the mystery, confusion and doubt before you put out that final cigarette and you know that:
- there is nothing to 'give up'
- smoking doesn't assist concentration and relaxation
- or relieve boredom and stress
- but is a major cause of boredom and stress and actually impedes concentration and relaxation.

Doesn't it make more sense to start off with awareness of the beautiful truth: that you are giving up nothing; that, far from being deprived of some pleasure or crutch, you are simply being cured of Western society's No.1 killer disease and a lifetime of misery, poverty and slavery? Doesn't it make more sense to start off with the feeling of:

ISN'T IT GREAT? I'M FREE!
I'M A NON-SMOKER!

That's what the hundreds of thousands of ex-smokers who have succeeded with Easyway did. All you need to do is to follow the instructions for it to happen to you. If you start off with that happy feeling, you don't have to wait for something to happen:

If you wait to feel like a non-smoker, whether it be for five days, three weeks or longer, you will simply be waiting to achieve a state that you are already in. In effect, you will be waiting for nothing to happen.

YOU ARE ALREADY A HAPPY NON-SMOKER

And you can get on with the rest of your life rejoicing in that fact. The effects of smoking never leave the body completely while there are smokers around. Even non-smokers have traces of it. Be assured, though, that the bulk of the gunge leaves your body within a few days of quitting.

Don't wait for it to happen! The moment you put out that final cigarette, you will quickly become stronger, both physically and mentally.

When you have a bad day, accept it. Just say to yourself, 'OK, I'm having one of those days, but because I am physically and mentally stronger, I'm better off than I was when I was smoking.'

You will soon discover that the bad days will occur less frequently and the good days will multiply.

Ready for anything

Just as non-smokers and smokers have good days and bad days, so do ex-smokers. With a 'willpower' method, the ex-smoker tends to blame everything that goes wrong on the fact that she no longer smokes. With Easyway, she expects things to go wrong but is aware that the moment she puts out that final cigarette, not only will the nicotine start to leave her body, but so will all the other bad effects.

That empty feeling

How will you distinguish between the death throes of the 'little monster' and a genuine hunger for food? You won't know, any more than you know while you remain a smoker. You don't need to know.

During that period, you are going to eat sensible meals and you are not going to pick at snacks between meals. In other words, if you get the empty feeling you can assume that it is the death throes. Rejoice in them.

The 'little monster' is real, but it never craves. Like the rest of the brainwashing, it might be the catalyst to making you crave a cigarette, but you have the choice of whether you do or don't continue to smoke.

Just as you have a choice whether or not to leave your hand under scalding hot water, you have exactly the same choice if you catch yourself thinking, 'I need a cigarette.'

Is it sensible to ponder the fact that you can't have one? If you do, what you are actually pondering is, 'Would I like to become addicted to Devastation?'

'Come to think of it, there's no point at all in smoking!'

CHAPTER 19

How many myths have we exploded?

Let's take stock of everything we've discussed so far. Consider each of the original questions put to you in the questionnaire on pages 65 and 66. Take your time and, when you are ready, make a note of your responses. When you have done this, compare them with the responses you gave before.

Are they different?

Now read the explanations that follow each of the questions below. Where necessary, refer back to relevant chapters to ensure you understand the points made.

1. Do smokers smoke because they choose to?

We have firmly established (Chapter 7) that smokers no more choose to smoke than they choose to speak their native tongue.

2. Do people smoke out of habit?

No, they smoke because they fell for the most subtle and ingenious trap that man and nature have combined to set for them: nicotine addiction (Chapter 5).

3. Are long-term smokers more hooked than teenagers? (Chapter 5)

When does the insect in the pitcher plant become trapped? The very moment it lands on the plant and starts to eat nectar.

Youngsters get hooked the very moment they light that first experimental cigarette.

4. Are heavy smokers more hooked than casual smokers? (Chapter 9)

'Darling, please, do I look like an addict?'

Who would you envy the most: someone trapped in quicksand up to her ankles or someone who is up to her neck in it?

They are both in the same trap and headed for the same destination although the victim, up to her ankles in it, is yet to realize her predicament. If you realise that you are in a trap and want to escape, at least you have a chance. But if you have no desire to escape, your chances are zero.

5. Do youngsters start smoking to feel adult, 'cool' or rebellious?

There is no doubt that youngsters do like to feel adult and 'cool'. Aren't childhood and adolescence just training grounds for adulthood?

A rebellious spirit is surely a quality rather than an evil, provided it has good intentions and receives good guidance. THERE ARE A MILLION AND ONE WAYS OF REALLY REBELLING OR REALLY BEING COOL. SMOKING DOESN'T REALLY COME CLOSE.

Our excuses for smoking keep changing, but the actual reason never does. The real reason is to try to end that empty, insecure feeling that the first cigarette created. Each new cigarette just prolongs it and guarantees that you suffer it again and again. But it doesn't have to be that way. Once you've removed the brainwashing and illusions about smoking, you will find it easy to be free!

Teenagers don't particularly admire grown-ups who smoke.

Shy youngsters admire their rebellious peers. Smoking is still adopted as a badge of independence, a form of cutting loose from parents, an integral part of the rite of passage into adulthood.

We all began smoking for a variety of foolish reasons. But that's absolutely no reason to carry on with it now. Youngsters actually started for the same reason we did...

They were conned!

I remember the pain of watching my father coughing his lungs up. There was nothing chic or 'cool' about his watering, bloodshot eyes, his nicotine-stained fingers and teeth or his bad breath. But did this prevent me from falling into the trap? Of course not.

6. Are smokers stupid?

If they are, that would make Sigmund Freud, Bertrand Russell and even Albert Einstein stupid.

Is a mouse stupid for nibbling at the cheese in a trap? Is an insect stupid for landing on a pitcher plant and drinking the nectar? If we say they are, it's only because we can see the trap and wouldn't fall for it ourselves.

But the nicotine trap is something else.

It's ingenious, designed by humans to attract humans.

- Just a few generations ago it had trapped 80 per cent of the adult male population.
- It still traps over 30 per cent of our youngsters, and now more girls than boys.
- It is responsible for the early death of more people than any other single disease, starvation and the combined war casualties of the history of our planet.
- Nicotine addiction currently claims over five million victims every year. The World Health Organization has estimated that the figure will rise to ten million by the second decade of this century.

Would you say a mouse is stupid for nibbling at the cheese in a trap?

Pass it on

Many years ago I was the only advocate for Easyway. Now there are tens of millions who can vouch for my claims that Easyway works. When you have satisfied yourself as to this fact, I would be grateful if you would do more than just write to thank me. Please contact the media, your doctor, your local politician and ask them why they persist in perpetuating the widescale illusions that enable this particular blight on our planet and its occupants to flourish. Share your happy news on social media. Let the world know how easy it is to be free.

Telling our children that smoking is expensive and bad for their health clearly doesn't prevent them from falling into the trap.

What will prevent them from falling into the trap is an explanation of exactly how the trap works. Simply telling them that smoking ruins their health won't dissuade them.

What greater gift can we pass on to our youngsters than the information that will give them at least a fighting chance of avoiding the nicotine trap?

Even rebellious youngsters are open to approaches that don't involve scare tactics.

7. Do smokers enjoy the taste of some cigarettes? (Chapter 5)
8. Do some cigarettes (e.g. after a meal) taste better than others?

In a recent survey, more than two-thirds of smokers admitted they had smoked butts out of an ashtray after running out of cigarettes. We don't smoke because of the taste; we learn to cope with the taste in order to get to the drugs to which we are addicted!

Some smokers claim to smoke because they enjoy the smell of tobacco, yet all smokers, when walking into a smoky atmosphere, will comment on how unpleasant it is.

In spite of the fact they don't like it, the effect can be particularly hazardous to ex-smokers at two key times, both of which you need to be aware of.

One is the first few days after you have put out your final cigarette.

The other is a social occasion, particularly over Christmas and New Year, when parties are rife.

Even if you did like the smell of cigarettes or cigarette smoke, that's not why you smoke. Some people like the smell of petrol or freshly baked bread, but that doesn't lead them to spend their lives outside petrol stations or bakeries.

If you have recently stopped smoking it can be disconcerting to find yourself suddenly, out of nowhere, recognizing that smell and it triggering a thought about smoking in your mind. It doesn't mean you want a cigarette; it just means your brain has forgotten that you've stopped.

If this happens and you try not to think about cigarettes – you will just think about them even more.

If I say, 'WHATEVER YOU DO, YOU MUSTN'T THINK ABOUT A BANANA,' you will almost certainly think about a banana! It doesn't matter if you think about cigarettes – even if you think, 'I WANT ONE' – it doesn't mean you really do.

Some people find this difficult to accept but it is true. Think about it for a moment.

If you were arguing with a friend, at the height of this argument you might think, 'I could kill you now,' but that doesn't mean you really could kill them. It doesn't make you a bad person. It is just a thought. It's what you do with the thought that matters.

When you come to smoke your final cigarette, focus on it. Be fully aware of the vile smell, the disgusting taste and, above all, the filth that you are breathing into your lungs. It's really not worth it, is it?

It is very much like if you, for example, parked your car in the same parking space every day for a year, at work or at home, and

Can you imagine how Nelson Mandela felt on leaving prison? You will feel the same euphoria at the end of this book

after a year your parking space was moved one space down. You wouldn't be surprised if you parked your car in the old parking space by accident!

When that happened – you wouldn't turn the engine off, throw your hands in the air and think to yourself, 'DAMN, I'M INFATUATED WITH THIS PARKING SPACE. I'M EMOTIONALLY ATTACHED TO IT. I CAN'T POSSIBLY PARK MY CAR IN THE NEW SPACE!'

In fact you would just re-park your car. It doesn't mean you want to park in one space rather than the other one. It just means that your brain has forgotten that your parking space has moved.

'It's really not worth it, is it?'

And that is all that happens when you smell (and think about) cigarettes, even if you think about them one night while you're out with friends who smoke.

IT DOESN'T MEAN YOU WANT ONE.

It just means your brain has forgotten that you've stopped, which after years of smoking isn't surprising.

At that point rather than worrying about it, or panicking about it, or trying not to think about it: you'll be ready to welcome it and understand that it's no different to parking your car in an old parking space. Allow yourself to smile about it – it's not a bad sign.

SO SHOULD YOU AVOID PASSIVE SMOKING?

NO!

Get it clear in your mind: it is not the 'little monster' that addicts you. What addicts you is the 'big monster': the belief that some pleasure or support can be got from feeding the 'little monster'.

The good news is there is absolutely no need for you to avoid smokers and smoking situations. You're not trying to give up living! In fact, you haven't even 'given up' smoking. There is nothing to give up.

Remember, you become a non-smoker the moment you extinguish your final cigarette

It is your opportunity to prove that you don't have to wait to become a happy non-smoker. You can enjoy life, including meals and other social events, immediately.

The moment you put out that final cigarette you will have solved the problem. You will have ceased to poison your body and will rapidly become physically and mentally stronger. You can start enjoying your life immediately, provided, of course, that you don't start moping for support or pleasure that never actually existed.

If the thought of a party without smoking still frightens you, make a point of attending one as soon as possible after you've smoked your final cigarette. Go with a feeling of eager anticipation, not a feeling of apprehension. Nothing bad will happen.

On the contrary, something exciting and marvellous is happening.

You are about to achieve what every smoker on the planet dreams of: **FREEDOM**.

'Freeing yourself from nicotine addiction is a great achievement.'

Other smokers will be expecting you to be complaining and miserable. Even when you are the only non-smoker present, every one of those smokers will be envying you. Some of them might be too scared to admit it. Some might blow smoke in your face or deliberately offer you a cigarette when they think you are off-guard.

Don't despise them; pity them.

You might find yourself on such a high that you forget you have stopped, and find yourself reaching for one of those cigarettes.

Don't worry!

All you did was hit the wipers instead of the horn. The mere fact that you had forgotten is a marvellous sign. What better proof could you have that not only can you enjoy life immediately, but your thoughts don't need to be obsessed by the fact that you no longer smoke?

'Stopping smoking is not going to make me miserable.'

A constant battle of bluff rages between smokers and ex-smokers who have 'given up' with a 'willpower' method.

When you stop with Easyway, you don't have to bluff

The ex-smokers will keep going on about how much healthier they feel and how much money they have saved and what a filthy, disgusting habit smoking is anyway.

The smokers will enthuse about the pleasure they receive, that the money is well spent and that they could step under a truck tomorrow.

When you stop with Easyway, you don't have to bluff. You have a 'Royal Straight Flush' and you know the smokers don't even have a pair of twos.

Partners in crime

If your partner also smokes, don't make the mistake of trying to persuade them to stop at the same time. You'll either lose them, or even if they go through the motions, they'll secretly want to undermine your success. Just enjoy your own freedom. When they realize that you are genuinely free, they'll join you of their own accord.

We have now exploded the first eight examples of brainwashing. Myths 9 to 12 inclusive are best dealt with collectively.

9. Does smoking help to relieve boredom?
10. Does smoking help you to concentrate?
11. Does smoking help you to relax?
12. Does smoking help to relieve stress?

Ask a smoker how the same cigarette can have completely opposite effects.

In fact, there is a very simple explanation.

When nicotine leaves a smoker's body it causes them to feel stressed and tense. If a smoker is in a genuinely stressful situation, such as a car accident, they will assume that the stress is due entirely to the accident.

When they light up and actually feel less distressed than a moment before, their brain is fooled into believing that the cigarette has partially relieved the genuine stress.

What they don't realize is that, even while smoking the

Even while smoking, smokers are actually more distressed than if they were non-smokers

cigarette, they are actually more distressed than if they were a non-smoker. This is because the cigarette only partially relieves the withdrawal syndrome.

When you light up because you are bored, do you suddenly think, 'My word, this is interesting!'?

In a relaxing situation, smokers cannot feel completely relaxed while they are in the grip of the 'itch'. This explains why even casual smokers tend to chain-smoke at parties.

The only reason we believe that smoking relieves boredom is because we tend to light up when we are bored. But boredom is a mental problem. When it occurs it's telling us that we have nothing interesting to occupy our minds.

When you light up because you are bored, do you suddenly think, 'My word, this is interesting! I breathe these cancerous fumes into my lungs and then breathe them out again. What jolly fun this is!'?

We don't go through this mental process even when we smoke the so-called 'special' cigarettes, such as the one after a meal.

Just as chewing gum doesn't relieve stress, but simply serves to emphasize your unrelaxed state, so smoking, far from relieving boredom, simply emphasizes the fact that you are bored.

Nicotine addiction is a major cause of boredom for several valid reasons:

- Because we believe it relieves boredom, it is the easy option and prevents us from seeking genuine solutions to boredom.
- Because it makes us feel lethargic and strains our finances, we don't have the energy or money to take up genuinely interesting pursuits.

Most important of all...

- Because we feel increasingly uncomfortable in situations in which we cannot smoke, we avoid those situations.

Why do smokers smoke when they are bored? Partly because they have been brainwashed to believe that smoking relieves boredom. Mainly, though, because while you have something to occupy your mind that doesn't involve stress or concentration, you won't be aware of that 'itch'.

So the best way to relieve boredom is to do something that occupies your mind. In other words, to concentrate on something. But smokers believe that they cannot concentrate without a cigarette.

Smokers have a permanent distraction: the 'itch'

What is the key to effective concentration? To remove all distractions. Smokers have a permanent distraction: the 'itch'. This is why most smokers will light up before making a phone call.

Again, lighting up only partially relieves the 'itch', so you are actually less able to concentrate than if you were a non-smoker.

If it is true that smoking aids concentration, why don't we make it compulsory for train drivers, pilots, surgeons etc. to smoke during working hours? Why are they positively forbidden to smoke during working hours?

Because the 'itch' is only partially satisfied when we light up, smoking actually impedes concentration. The degeneration that nicotine sets in motion affects every organ, including the brain.

Is it only smokers and ex-smokers who experience mental blocks? If it is, smoking would appear to cause them rather than relieve them. After I stopped smoking with Easyway, I continued to get mental blocks, but because I knew that smoking ruins concentration, I didn't waste time moping for a cigarette. I put my mind to searching for a true solution to the block.

> Ask a smoker what it is they actually enjoy about breathing filthy, cancerous fumes into their lungs and they immediately become less effusive. Smoking is equivalent to wearing tight shoes; neither experience is enjoyable.

We have now exploded myths 1–12. Time to deal with two of the most enduring fantasies in the smoker's imagination.

13. Do smokers enjoy smoking?

Even when you understand the nature of the trap and how the illusion works, it is very difficult to comprehend that there is not a single smoker, past or present, who has enjoyed smoking a single cigarette, cigar or pipe.

You have to remove the illusions and all the brainwashing to come face to face with the true situation: that nicotine addiction is no more or less than Devastation, as defined at the beginning of Chapter 6.

Re-read that definition and you'll find it difficult to comprehend how anyone could be deluded into believing that they did enjoy smoking. However, there is one reason occasionally offered by the more discerning smokers as their reason for smoking:

THE RITUAL

If it were the ritual that was so pleasurable, it would be possible to continue with the ritual but not actually light the cigarette.

Smokers have tried doing this but found that it only works for a short period. It's easy to understand why it doesn't work if you appreciate the ritual of eating.

Imagine going to a lovely restaurant with a pleasant atmosphere and a picturesque view. It's all there: the clean linen, cut-glass, silver and china. A waiter shows you and your friends to your seats and you study the menu, enjoying the wonderful aromas coming from the kitchen.

Finally the food arrives. You are about to taste the first mouthful when the waiter taps you politely on the shoulder and says, 'So sorry, but you're only paying for the ritual, not the food.'

'Smoking is no longer going to make me miss out on the real pleasures of life.'

The whole object of the ritual of a meal is to enhance your pleasure at satisfying your hunger. If you are not allowed to do that, the ritual becomes pointless and exceedingly frustrating.

The ritual of smoking would be pointless without being allowed to scratch that 'itch'

With smoking, the attractive shiny packaging, gold lighters, silver cigarette cases and cut-glass ashtrays serve the opposite purpose: to delude you into believing that there is something pleasant or sociable in breathing filthy, cancerous fumes into your lungs.

Just as the ritual of a meal would be pointless without being allowed to eat, so the ritual of smoking would be pointless without being allowed to scratch that 'itch'.

14. Do some people have addictive personalities?

You cannot prove that something doesn't exist. But you can weigh all the evidence, use your intelligence and decide which is the more likely possibility.

Many smokers come to the conclusion that they have an addictive personality. Why? Usually because it's the only rational explanation they can think of for continuing to do something that they know is destroying their health and wealth.

If I were to commission you to research why more Egyptians than Ukrainians drown in the Nile, and to establish whether the Egyptians have a personality trait which causes them to drown in the Nile, it wouldn't take you long to come up with a sensible conclusion. Ukrainians don't drown in the Nile because they don't live near it.

The Egyptians don't have an addiction to drowning; they drown only when bathing in or boating on the Nile.

Equally, the simple reason why you are not addicted to heroin is that you don't use it.

You can't be addicted to anything unless you use it first.

Amazingly this is a revelation to thousands of smokers who believed they had addictive personalities until they tried Easyway.

It's not your personality that addicts you, but an addictive drug

What also addicts you is the belief that you get pleasure and/or support from the drug, and that you cannot enjoy life or cope with stress without that drug.

Once this illusion is exploded, so is the addiction.

We have now exploded myths 1–14 inclusive. Soon we will move on to the remaining six.

CHAPTER 20

Removing the associations

Easyway will work for any smoker. But, no matter how hard we try, there is a small percentage of smokers who don't succeed. Although they might refer to themselves as failures, we never do. We know that each one of them can find it easy to stop. Our motto is the same as that of the Canadian Mounties: 'We Always Get Our Man' – or Woman!

In all cases where success is proving difficult, we attempt to analyse the reasons. Please pay particular attention to the following points, which appear to be the main reasons for failure:

1. **The belief that you are different and that Easyway won't work for you.**

You are no different from any of the other 40 per cent of the world's population who fell into the trap

This is negative thinking, pure and simple, and will defeat you before you start. You are no different from any of the other 40 per cent of the world's population who fell into the trap and are trying to escape, except in one important respect: you are now in possession of the true facts.

2. **Starting in a depressed and fearful frame of mind, believing that stopping is going to be very difficult.**

'Taste? Cigarettes killed my sense of taste years ago!'

What is there to be depressed about? You are choosing to be free after years of slavery. Start off in a happy, confident frame of mind and see stopping as an exciting challenge. You have absolutely nothing to lose and so much to gain.

3. **Not understanding that the only reason any smoker continues to smoke is to feed the 'little monster'.**

The notion that smoking gives you either pleasure or support is simply an illusion created by the 'little monster'. You understand the chain of deception now, and realize that when you light up, each cigarette, far from removing the empty, insecure feeling, actually perpetuates it. The permanent cure is to get rid of the monster altogether.

4. **Not understanding that the 'little monster' will survive for a few days after you put out your final cigarette.**

Any craving you feel after you've put out your final cigarette is just the 'little monster' in its death throes. Enjoy feeling it die and rejoice in your decision to stop.

5. **Failure to recognize and then break down the associations with smoking.**

There are dozens of associations that can make it impossible to escape the trap if we don't recognize them and break them. Let's address a few of the more typical ones:

The vacation

You meet a crowd of smokers on holiday. They're all having a good time. The cigarettes are passed around and it's easy to think, 'This isn't fair; these people are obviously having a good time. They can smoke and I can't.'

Of course they are having a good time: they're on holiday! Although they won't all admit it, every one of those smokers will be envying you. You're on holiday AND you're not chained to smoking.

The flight delay

You are bored and frustrated and you can hear smokers gloating over the money they've saved buying duty-frees. It's easy to sit there thinking, 'I used to save a fortune on duty-frees. I'll just buy the one packet.'

Instead, remind yourself that on average those smokers are going to spend tens of thousands in their lifetime, just for the privilege of enslaving themselves and destroying their health.

The trauma

Someone crashes into your car. You start to think, 'At times like this I would have had my little crutch.'

Think back to the time when you were a smoker and had mini-dramas, or major ones for that matter. No doubt you did light a cigarette, probably several, but can you ever remember thinking, 'Isn't life wonderful? I've smashed up my lovely car, but who cares? I've got this gorgeous cigarette to smoke.'

Smoking doesn't relieve the pain of such situations, it simply adds another agony.

The reunion

You and a friend have been in the habit of reminiscing about past experiences and getting up to date with current progress, all with the aid of a glass of wine and a cigarette. How could it possibly be the same without the cigarette?

Prepare yourself for such situations in advance. Never forget that, no matter how your friend might try to convince you otherwise, she would love to be free, like you. Your success could just be the key that frees her. Imagine the satisfaction you would feel!

'True misery is the feeling that you must have a cigarette.'

Expect to find yourself in situations where old associations present themselves. If and when those bells do start ringing, reinforce your decision by understanding that your first reaction – 'I want a cigarette' – is nothing more than a conditioned reflex, like parking your car in an old parking space.

Smokers tend to stress the negative aspects of not being able to smoke. We can't imagine being able to cope with or enjoy certain situations without a cigarette.

This is because we associate being miserable with not having cigarettes. The fear of being miserable forever in ALL situations is enough to put anyone off even attempting to stop smoking.

REMEMBER

– you're not going to be miserable.
You are going to feel

FREE

You don't have to wait to become a non-smoker, or even endure a period of misery

It's not only the 'little monster' that triggers 'I want or need a cigarette!' Any of the associations we've discussed will do it.

Get it clearly into your mind that all those situations you associate with smoking were intrinsically pleasant before you started smoking, and will be again.

Remember that your smoking actually impeded your pleasure at such times, because of the learned pattern of behaviour that only addicts suffer from.

If smoking could do everything that smokers claim it does, would you not agree that, right up until your final cigarette, you would have been;

TOTALLY Stress-free

ALWAYS Relaxed

NEVER Bored and

ABLE to concentrate at all times?

'I'm getting genuinely excited about quitting. Can I put this out now?'

Who was it who created the expectation that somehow we were missing something that we needed to make us complete?

The sixth and greatest reason why some smokers do not achieve initial success with Easyway is what we call the Void.

CHAPTER 21

The Void

How often have you heard that old phrase, 'Schooldays are the happiest days of your life'? Try telling that to a teenage girl facing exams, at the same time as coping with the physical changes of adolescence, the changing relationship with parents and the social pressures of friendship, romance etc.

Every stage of life has its stresses and strains, right from the moment we're born, yet whatever stage of life we're at, we always yearn for a former time, when we perceive life to have been so much easier.

Why?

Because we are programmed to feel that there is a hole in our lives that makes us incomplete:

The Void

What is 'the Void'?

It is the belief that, by whichever means we evolved on this planet, somehow we are incomplete.

The Void is enlarged by brainwashing and disillusionment.

Life is a series of disillusionments:

*
Fairy tales aren't real

*
Parents aren't infallible

*
People can be cruel

*
Heroes can fail

*
And so on...

Every disillusionment leaves a void, and so we continually search for the miracle that will make us feel complete.

Enter the tobacco industry.

Pulling the wool over your eyes

Seizing on the knowledge that people desire and acquire products to boost themselves, the tobacco companies hired eminent psychoanalysts to work closely with marketing departments to come up with the right image to fit the desires of their potential market. This work is still going on, as the tobacco companies are still succeeding in trapping generations of smokers. Of course, one of their priority targets is young women and girls.

Tobacco industry market research revealed that women seem to be less influenced by anti-smoking campaigns, mainly because these are perceived to be geared towards male smokers.

- In the 1960s the ratio of male to female smokers stood at 60:40.
- Since then the trend has been towards parity.
- By 1998, 28 per cent of men and 27 per cent of women were smokers.

The tobacco companies have turned their attention to snaring more women. The proportion of smokers among women now equals that of men.

Among teenagers the rate for girls is rising fast, and in some countries they are actually out-smoking the boys.

The tobacco industry clearly regards women as a separate market to be conquered and a large portion of the annual advertising and marketing budget is aimed in their direction. An enormous amount of research has gone into targeting this market.

'Sometimes it's better not to compete with men!'

The 'healthy' option

If you smoke any brand that flies under the banner of 'lights', you've been well and truly had. This product was aimed at the health conscious and designed to represent a major step in reducing harm, thus providing the smoker with an apparently legitimate reason not to stop. Without much prompting, the tobacco companies concede that these cigarettes 'are nothing more than a scam'. You just take in deeper breaths, inhale more often and hold the smoke down longer. It's proven that in this way smokers manage to extract the same level of toxins from light cigarettes as from any other type.

How Big Tobacco sees you

The chart opposite shows how tobacco companies have psychoanalysed the female market, all the better to understand where the opportunities lie and how best to target them. I've no doubt you can spot yourself in one of the categories.

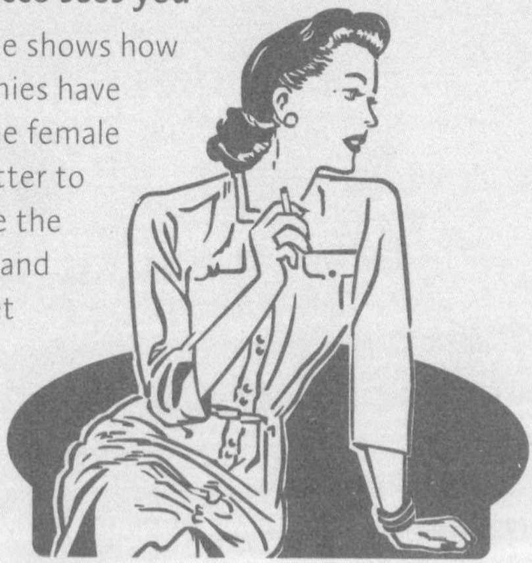

How Big Tobacco sees you

Information taken from *'A Structural/Psychological Segmentation of the Adult Female Market'* (market research commissioned by a leading tobacco company)

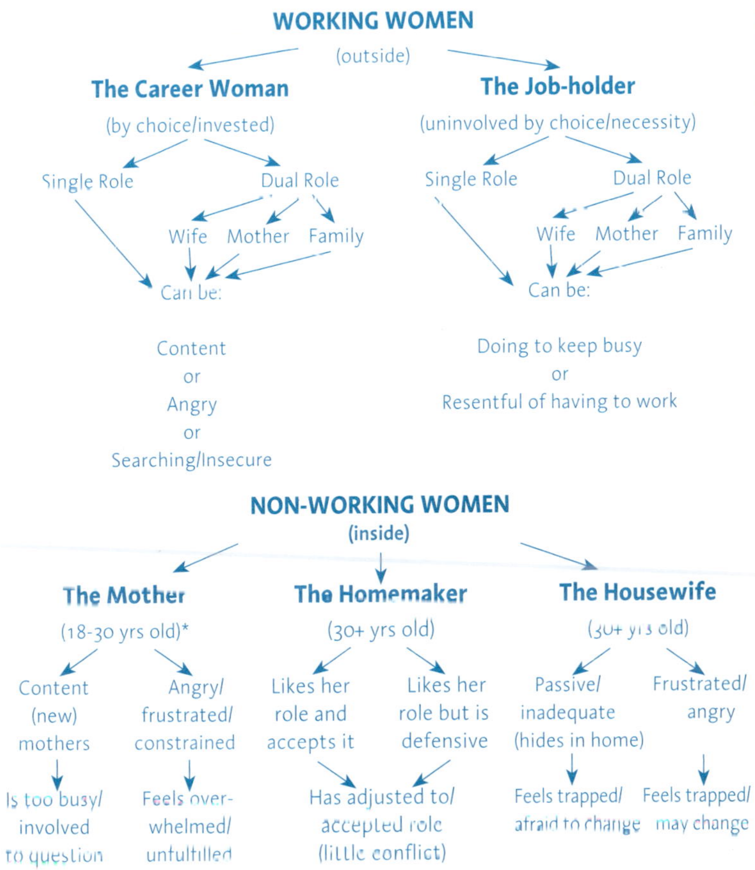

* The ages are given as reference points only. There are fewer and fewer women aged 18-30 who do not have children and are not in paid employment

The tobacco companies have even developed products specifically aimed at women on low incomes. What better than a flash of gold on a packet to give the illusion of grandeur and wealth?

You can now use this information to reinforce the new perception you have of cigarettes, to keep you from getting back into the prison that the chart illustrates so clearly.

You have lived through the reality of being a smoker. You didn't like it and wanted to escape; that's why you are reading this book. Being a smoker can never get better, only worse. If you hate the position you're in now, you'll always hate it.

If you could go back in time to that very first cigarette, what advice would you give yourself? No doubt, you'd shout, 'Don't do it.'

You will soon be in the unique position when you put out that final cigarette, when you end the nightmare and walk free. You will take yourself back to a time when you could enjoy life as if you had never lit that first cigarette. With all that you know now, you can give yourself the best advice. At last you can make an informed choice.

YOU CAN STAY IN THE TRAP FOR THE REST

OF YOUR LIFE, IGNORING THE REALITY

99 PER CENT OF THE TIME, KNOWING

HOW MISERABLE YOU ARE AND

WILL ALWAYS BE

or

YOU CAN SET YOURSELF FREE AND CELEBRATE THE JOY OF ESCAPE

Human beings are the most physically and mentally complete creatures on Earth. Our nagging sense of incompleteness is the result of brainwashing and that is a uniquely human function, made possible by our intellect.

Just as the power of reason can be used to hoodwink us into wanting things we don't need or that are bad for us, it can also be used to protect us from the brainwashing.

In fact, it works more powerfully in our favour. Once you see through an illusion, you cannot be fooled by it again.

Just as you quickly adjust to the changes in your new car, you are quickly going to reverse the habit of seeing a cigarette as relieving the empty feeling, and feeling deprived because you can't have one.

You have no more need or desire to smoke. Neither do you need anything in its place.

This leads us back to the questionnaire, and Illusion 17: Does it help to use nicotine gum, patches or sprays?

Let me now explain exactly why all substitutes make it harder to stop.

The never-ending itch

Since the day you smoked your first cigarette, you have been trying to fill a void artificially created in you by that cigarette, not realizing that, far from filling the void, it temporarily fills part of it and then goes on to create a new void.

CHAPTER 22

Substitutes

Let's focus on what we are achieving: never to have the need or desire to smoke another cigarette. You might still believe that it is difficult to obtain that state. I promise you that it is simplicity itself, providing you follow all the instructions.

One of the instructions is not to use any substitutes whatsoever.

If you search for a substitute, what you are saying to yourself is, 'I know smoking is ruining my health and wealth and I'd like to be rid of that side of it, but it was also my pleasure and support and I need something to take its place.'

By saying this, you are simply confirming that you believe that you are dependent upon the drug.

> When you recover from a bout of flu, do you search for another disease to take its place? Of course you don't, you are just happy to know that you are over it. Now re-read the definition of Devastation in Chapter 6; that's the disease you've been suffering from.

The quicker you can starve the 'little monster' the better, so the quicker you can remove the 'big monster' the better. Fortunately, the 'big monster' is purely a figment of your imagination and the 'little monster' is weak.

All substitutes by design prolong the life of the 'big monster'. Substitutes that contain nicotine, like nicotine gum, patches and nasal sprays, have the added disadvantage of prolonging the life of the 'little monster' too.

Here's the theory behind using substitutes; see if you can spot the holes.

When you attempt to 'give up' smoking, you have two powerful adversaries to defeat. One is the terrible physical pains caused by withdrawal from nicotine; the other is the habit itself. Isn't it just common sense to tackle one adversary at a time?

So, after you put out what you hope will be your final cigarette, while you are breaking the habit, you keep your body supplied with nicotine to avoid the terrible physical withdrawal symptoms. Then, having broken the habit, you can face the second adversary, and ease the problem by gradually cutting down on the intake of nicotine.

I have asked dozens of qualified doctors, 'How is it possible to help cure a drug addict by prescribing the same drug that the victim is addicted to?' Not only has not one of them attempted to offer an explanation, but it hadn't even occurred to any of them that that was what they were actually doing!

Nicotine Replacement Therapy (NRT) may appear logical at first glance but it is based on three false assumptions:

1. That smoking is a habit.
2. That habits are difficult to break.
3. That the withdrawal of nicotine creates severe physical withdrawal pains.

We have already exploded all three of these assumptions.

To advise a smoker not to smoke but to chew gum that contains nicotine is equivalent to advising a heroin addict not to smoke heroin but to inject it straight into a vein!

Even the phrase 'Nicotine Replacement Therapy' is a misnomer. There is no therapy involved and there isn't any replacement.

'When I stop, will you stop too? We'll both be a lot happier, you know.'

> We have literally thousands of ex-smokers attend our clinics in order to be released from addiction to nicotine gum.

What are we searching for when we seek a substitute? Something that has all the advantages of smoking without the downside? A 'magic' pill that will relieve boredom and improve concentration, that is both a stimulant and a relaxant?

Come on! Do you still believe in fairies? Isn't that why you fell into the trap in the first place?

Your body and brain don't need outside help. Sure, they won't eliminate genuine stress any more than a cigarette will, but they will ensure you get adrenaline on demand to enable you to cope with stress, and they will provide dopamines to relax you and make you feel happy when the danger has passed.

> As products such as e-cigarettes and other smokeless nicotine products become more and more widespread, don't kid yourself that they are any better than NRT or even smoking. They will still keep you hooked, control your life, make you poor and destroy your health.

So, we are left with just the four final illusions on the questionnaire:

17. Does it take willpower to stop?
18. Is it necessary to suffer from physical withdrawal symptoms?
19. Do ex-smokers have to endure an initial period of craving and irritability?
20. Is it difficult to stop?

We have already partially addressed all four points. The answer to them all is an emphatic 'No' – provided you have followed all the instructions.

You have now reached an exciting stage. You are in sight of achieving your goal.

Do you feel a little nervous and anxious?

Don't worry about that. All you need do is to follow the final instructions.

CHAPTER 23

The final instructions

Before we go ahead with the final instructions, there is one important subject that we haven't discussed: TIMING.

You may be asking yourself, 'Is now really the right time to attempt to stop?' Please don't fall into that ingenious trap. It will have you thinking there is never a right time.

Supposing someone was suffering from a disease that would get progressively worse and there was a simple and inexpensive cure to that disease. When would you advise them to apply the cure? You don't even have to think about it. The answer is, and always has been, NOW! NOW! NOW!

Nothing bad is happening. On the contrary, something marvellous is happening:

GO FOR IT!

What sort of idiot would you have thought Edmund Hillary if, having got to within 100 feet of the summit of Everest, he had ummed and ahhed and finally concluded, 'Perhaps I should wait until next year'?

Very soon you are going to undertake the ritual of the final cigarette. Before you do, it is imperative that you fully understand the vital cornerstone on which Easyway is based: that smoking gives you no genuine pleasure or support, in any shape or form.

Smoking gives you no genuine pleasure or support

I do not mean that the disadvantages of being a smoker far outweigh any advantages. Every smoker knows this.

I mean there are NO advantages.

In addition, you need to understand that this scenario applies to every smoker, and not just to you.

If you are not clear about these two points, re-read the book and do not to attempt to stop until you are. If you continue to find difficulty, you can obtain further assistance from any Easyway clinic (see the listing at the back of the book).

Smoking is a total waste of time. There are no advantages to being a smoker

The staff at my clinics around the world are always happy to provide a free word of advice or support to anyone who has read one of my books.

If you have tried to stop in the past and found it difficult or impossible, you might not readily accept the idea that any smoker can find it easy and enjoyable.

The proof of the pudding is in the eating – and some people need to eat the pudding first! Here are your final instructions:

1. Check your frame of mind

Remember, the real difference between a smoker and a non-smoker is not that one smokes and the other doesn't; it is that a non-smoker has no need or desire to smoke – not today, not tomorrow, not ever.

If you find the thought of never, ever smoking another cigarette difficult to face, try thinking about the alternatives and how they make you feel:

- Going through life craving a cigarette but not allowing yourself to have one

or

- Never being allowed to stop smoking.

It is essential that you start off – and continue – in a happy frame of mind; that you see smoking as it really is (a drug called DEVASTATION); and that you realize you are about to achieve something marvellous:

Release from the slavery of nicotine addiction

2. Make a positive decision to stop

You never decided to become a smoker for life. Like every other smoker, you were lured into the trap. You won't escape just by hoping that some day you'll be released by some miracle. You have to make a positive decision to escape.

There are no pros or cons to weigh up

The decision you are making is not whether to stop smoking. You have the wonderful choice of deciding whether you spend the rest of your life in the trap or being free of it.

In truth, there are absolutely no pros or cons to weigh up. There are no advantages whatsoever to being a smoker. The disadvantages are so hideous that, once hooked, we cannot bear even to think about them.

I want you to make a solemn vow now: that when you have completed the ritual of smoking the final cigarette, no matter what happens in your life, you will never smoke another cigarette.

3. **Having made what you know to be the correct choice, never, ever question or doubt your decision.**

If it has been some days since you smoked your final cigarette, just confirm to yourself that you have already smoked your final one. If you are using any type of nicotine product, have one last puff, suck, or whatever!

We've been brainwashed from birth to see smoking as a pleasure and/or support. Your perception of smoking has been distorted. It can become so again. But the facts have never altered. Smoking is nothing more or less than addiction to Devastation.

Allowing yourself to doubt your decision means allowing yourself one of only two choices.

1. To resist the temptation to smoke and feel miserable and deprived.
2. To go on being a slave to nicotine and feeling even more miserable.

Allow yourself the third choice:

3. To accept that you've been brainwashed, rejoice in the fact that you now understand the trap, you know that smoking does absolutely nothing for you, and every time the thought of smoking enters your mind, revel in that knowledge and the realization that you are free.

You have achieved something that every smoker on the planet would dearly love to achieve.

Your perception of smoking has been distorted. It can become so again

THE RITUAL OF YOUR FINAL CIGARETTE

You have been in training for this moment all of your smoking life: to put out a cigarette. You've set out to achieve something that society in general believes to be very difficult and that many smokers are certain is impossible. Having got this far, you aren't just close to success, you have already completed the course.

The ritual of the final cigarette is rather like the pomp and circumstance of the Oscar ceremony. Would an Oscar be quite so important without the ceremony?

See the ritual of the final cigarette as it really is: a ceremony dedicated to you for your personal glorification to celebrate your release and escape from a nightmarish slavery: nicotine addiction.

'I really can do it. I'm never going to smoke another of these things again.'

You can, of course, choose to complete the ceremony in the company of your close family and friends. You might, however, prefer to complete it in private.

For those of you who have followed my instructions and have continued to smoke until this point, **I WOULD LIKE YOU TO SMOKE YOUR FINAL CIGARETTE NOW**.

If you have already smoked your final cigarette, this mustn't prevent you from celebrating your achievement. In fact, it is essential that you do so now, even though you are already ahead of the game.

However you choose to carry out the ritual, be conscious of smoking that final cigarette.

Be aware that there is nothing pleasurable about the taste and that there is something decidedly unpleasant about breathing bad, cancerous fumes into your lungs.

Be aware that if you choose to go through the ceremony alone, your close family and friends will still be rooting for you.

In fact, although they might not admit it, every smoker on the planet will be rooting for you, because every time someone like you manages to escape from the trap, it gives hope to those left in its grips.

One enjoyable cigarette

Contrary to what I've said all along, it *is* possible not only to enjoy smoking one cigarette but to be filled with ecstasy by smoking it – provided, of course, that you understand that it is your last cigarette!

When you have put out that final cigarette, be aware that you are already a non-smoker. All you need to do from this point on is to accept that smokers, just like non-smokers and ex-smokers, have good days and bad days.

Expect to feel somewhat disorientated for a few days, but don't worry about it: that's simply a sign that you are recovering.

All you need to do from this point on, whenever you think about smoking, whether you are having a good day or a bad day, is not to question your decision, but think:

YIPPEE, I'M A NON-SMOKER!

In the meantime, just follow all the instructions and in a few days you will soon enjoy a wonderful experience:

THE 'MOMENT OF REVELATION'.

The ingenuity of the trap has conditioned you to believe that any empty, insecure feeling can be partly relieved by smoking a cigarette. The whole purpose of Easyway is to help you understand that the complete opposite is the truth. It takes time to adjust to this truth.

The 'Moment of Revelation' is similar to the feeling you get when you swim for the first time without water wings, learn to ride a bike unaided, or when you pass your driving test. The real joy of these moments comes out of the achiever's sense of new-found freedom.

The 'Moment of Revelation' far exceeds any of these examples.

This special moment usually occurs a few days after you have stopped, after one of those situations that you thought you couldn't enjoy or handle without a cigarette. Afterwards it dawns on you: not only did you get through without needing to smoke, but you never even thought about smoking!

Then you realize that everything I've been saying is true:

- social occasions *can* be more pleasant
- you are *better* equipped to handle stress
- you *don't* have to spend the rest of your life feeling that you are missing out
- the expression 'once a smoker, always a smoker' is nonsense.

Afterwards it dawns on you: you never even thought about smoking!

Just as trying not to think about smoking will create a phobia and guarantee that you'll never stop thinking about it, so trying to create the 'Moment of Revelation' will guarantee that you never achieve it.

Smokers using a 'willpower' method rarely have that moment of revelation because they are never sure they have succeeded.

If your objective is to stop smoking for a week or a year, you cannot possibly know that you have succeeded until the week or year has passed.

On the same basis, if your objective is never to smoke again, you won't know whether or not you have succeeded until your life is over. In effect, you will never know.

So how will you know with Easyway?

Because you understand the nature of the trap.

You are already a non-smoker. The nightmare is over. The main objective of this book wasn't to help you to stop smoking. It was to enable you to enjoy life more. Get on and do just that!

Don't worry if you don't quickly experience the 'Moment of Revelation'. If you have followed all the instructions, you will already be a happy non-smoker.

Quitting smoking will inspire confidence and belief in yourself

A small minority of ex-smokers find it relatively easy to stop with Easyway and are quite happy to remain non-smokers, but do not experience the 'Moment of Revelation'. This is because they have failed to follow all of the instructions.

They haven't broken all the associations.

Quitting smoking is regarded as an incredibly difficult goal to achieve. Once you achieve it, the confidence and belief in yourself that it inspires enables you to confront and control aspects of your life that previously caused you concern.

This is the greatest of the many advantages that being free of nicotine confers.

'Moment of Revelation? Do you really think it can work for me?'

CHAPTER 24

How to remain a happy non-smoker for the rest of your life

By far the biggest tragedy with Easyway is not failure to succeed initially, but succeeding and then getting hooked again. This final chapter is an attempt to ensure that doesn't happen to you.

If Easyway has a weakness it is the temptation to become blasé. Because it makes stopping so easy, clients can become over-confident.

By the end of the course, the smoker knows there are many powerful and valid reasons never to smoke again, and not a single valid reason to continue. But over time the bad side of smoking is forgotten.

The reason I wanted you to write your 'Personal Record' was so that you could refer to it occasionally and remind yourself of exactly why it is great to be free.

> The danger isn't so much in the early days when you can remember how much you hated being a smoker. One of the kindnesses of Mother Nature is that generally she allows us to remember the good times and forget the tragedies. Sadly, this can backfire on us. Always remember how hideous smoking is.

Make sure you record your feelings when you receive the 'Moment of Revelation'.

Unless you have completely removed the brainwashing and are clear in your mind that you have no need or desire to smoke, you will remain vulnerable to falling back into the trap.

It is easy to stop immediately and permanently, but never underestimate the ingenuity of the trap. You have made a solemn vow never, ever to smoke another cigarette. The most important instruction of Easyway is:

HAVING MADE WHAT YOU KNOW TO BE THE CORRECT DECISION, NEVER, EVER DOUBT OR QUESTION THAT DECISION.

Whenever you think about smoking from now on and for the rest of your life, just remind yourself:

YIPPEE, I'M A NON-SMOKER!

Just as initial success is guaranteed, provided you follow all the instructions, so permanent success is also guaranteed. Any smoker who fails to stop initially or permanently with Easyway does so not because Easyway didn't work for them, but because they failed to follow all the instructions.

If you do have a problem, either now or in the future, just refer to The Principal Instructions to Follow While Reading This Book (below).

Read through them now. Don't just skip over each item, thinking, 'Yes, that's obvious.' You've worked so hard getting this far, it would be a shame to ruin it all by being blasé.

Treat each item seriously. Ask yourself, do I really believe this point? Do I really understand it?

Congratulations! You have freed yourself from the nicotine trap. You are now a Happy Non-smoker.

HAVE FUN!

The Principal Instructions To Follow While Reading This Book

1. Keep an open mind, page 68
2. Maintain a happy frame of mind throughout, page 69
3. Make no attempt to stop or cut down before finishing the book, page 70
4. Have patience: don't jump the gun, page 70
5. Record your Personal Statement, page 71

THE INSTRUCTIONS TO FOLLOW THAT MAKE IT EASY TO STOP PERMANENTLY

1. Keep this book safely in a place where you can easily refer to it. Do not lose it, lend it out or give it away.

2. Never forget that smoking confers no advantages whatsoever on you or any other smoker.

3. Never envy other smokers. They'll be envying you. You are not being deprived. They are.

4. Remember you did not enjoy being a smoker. That's why you stopped. You do enjoy being a non-smoker.

5. Be aware that the 'little monster' will survive for a few days and that you might find yourself reaching for a cigarette. If this happens, don't worry about it. Use the moment to remind yourself just how nice it is to be free.

6. Remember, there is no such thing as just one cigarette.

7. Enjoy breaking the associations. Make a point of finding them to destroy them.

8. Don't use substitutes – you don't need them.

9. Accept that you'll have good days and bad, but never forget that the good days will be better and the bad days less so and fewer.

10. Don't avoid smoking situations or change your lifestyle just because you've stopped smoking, unless you wish to change it for purely selfish reasons. Remember: you've only stopped smoking, not living!

11. Do not attempt to cut down or to control your intake.

12. Re-read your Personal Statement. Keep it somewhere safe and refer to it every now and then.

13. Ignore the advice of 'experts' and friends if it contradicts these instructions, no matter how eminent these people are or how impressive they sound.

14. Don't wait for the 'Moment of Revelation' or to feel like you have become a non-smoker – you are already one. Just get on with your life.

15. If you have any difficulties, contact your nearest Allen Carr clinic. You will find a list of those on the following pages.

16. Don't try not to think about smoking. Whenever it comes into your mind, tell yourself, 'Yippee, I'm a non-smoker!'

17. ABOVE ALL, HAVING MADE WHAT YOU KNOW TO BE THE CORRECT DECISION, NEVER QUESTION OR DOUBT IT.

ALLEN CARR'S EASYWAY CLINICS

The following pages list contact details for all Allen Carr's Easyway To Stop Smoking Clinics worldwide where the success rate, based on the three-month, money-back guarantee, is over 90%.

Selected clinics also offer sessions that deal with alcohol and weight issues. Please check with your nearest clinic, listed below, for details.

Allen Carr's Easyway guarantee that you will find it easy to stop smoking at the clinics or your money back.

LONDON CLINIC AND WORLDWIDE HEAD OFFICE
Park House, 14 Pepys Road,
Raynes Park, London SW20 8NH
Tel: +44 (0)20 8944 7761
Fax: +44 (0)20 8944 8619
Email: mail@allencarr.com
Website: www.allencarr.com
Therapists: John Dicey, Colleen Dwyer, Crispin Hay, Emma Hudson, Rob Fielding

Worldwide Press Office
Contact: John Dicey
Tel: +44 (0)7970 88 44 52
Email: jd@allencarr.com

UK Clinic Information and Central Booking Line
Tel: 0800 389 2115

UK CLINICS

Aylesbury
Tel: 0800 0197 017
Therapists: Kim Bennett, Emma Hudson
Email: kim@easywaybucks.co.uk
Website: www.allencarr.com

Belfast
Tel: 0845 094 3244
Therapist: Tara Evers-Cheung
Email: tara@easywayni.com
Website: www.allencarr.com

Birmingham
Tel & Fax: +44 (0)121 423 1227
Therapists: John Dicey, Colleen Dwyer,
Crispin Hay, Rob Fielding
Email: info@allencarr.com
Website: www.allencarr.com

Bournemouth
Tel: 0800 028 7257
Therapists: John Dicey,
Colleen Dwyer, Emma Hudson
Email: info@allencarr.com
Website: www.allencarr.com

Brighton
Tel: 0800 028 7257
Therapists: John Dicey, Colleen Dwyer,
Emma Hudson
Email: info@allencarr.com
Website: www.allencarr.com

Bristol
Tel: +44 (0)117 950 1441
Therapist: Charles Holdsworth Hunt
Email:
stopsmoking@easywaybristol.co.uk
Website: www.allencarr.com

Cambridge
Tel: 0800 0197 017
Therapists: Kim Bennett,
Emma Hudson
Email: kim@easywaybucks.co.uk
Website: www.allencarr.com

Cardiff
Tel: +44 (0)117 950 1441
Therapist: Charles Holdsworth Hunt
Email:
stopsmoking@easywaybristol.co.uk
Website: www.allencarr.com

Coventry
Tel: 0800 321 3007
Therapist: Rob Fielding
Email: info@easywaycoventry.co.uk
Website: www.allencarr.com

Crewe
Tel: +44 (0)1270 664176
Therapist: Debbie Brewer-West
Email:
debbie@easyway2stopsmoking.co.uk
Website: www.allencarr.com

Cumbria
Tel: 0800 077 6187
Therapist: Mark Keen
Email: mark@easywaycumbria.co.uk
Website: www.allencarr.com

Derby
Tel: +44 (0)1270 664176
Therapists: Debbie Brewer-West
Email:
debbie@easyway2stopsmoking.co.uk
Website: www.allencarr.com

Exeter
Tel: +44 (0)117 950 1441
Therapist: Charles Holdsworth Hunt
Email:
stopsmoking@easywayexeter.co.uk
Website: www.allencarr.com

Guernsey
Tel: 0800 077 6187
Therapist: Mark Keen
Email:
mark@easywaylancashire.co.uk
Website: www.allencarr.com

High Wycombe
Tel: 0800 0197 017
Therapists: Kim Bennett, Emma Hudson
Email: kim@easywaybucks.co.uk
Website: www.allencarr.com

Isle of Man
Tel: 0800 077 6187
Therapist: Mark Keen
Email:
mark@easywaylancashire.co.uk
Website: www.allencarr.com

Jersey
Tel: 0800 077 6187
Therapist: Mark Keen
Email:
mark@easywaylancashire.co.uk
Website: www.allencarr.com

Kent
Tel: 0800 028 7257
Therapists: John Dicey, Colleen Dwyer, Emma Hudson
Email: info@allencarr.com
Website: www.allencarr.com

Lancashire
Tel: 0800 077 6187
Therapist: Mark Keen
Email:
mark@easywaylancashire.co.uk
Website: www.allencarr.com

Leeds
Tel: 0800 804 6796
Therapist: Rob Groves
Email: info@easywayyorkshire.co.uk
Website: www.allencarr.com

Leicester
Tel: 0800 321 3007
Therapist: Rob Fielding
Email: info@easywayleicester.co.uk
Website: www.allencarr.com

Liverpool
Tel: 0800 077 6187
Therapist: Mark Keen
Email:
mark@easywaylivorpool.co.uk
Website: www.allencarr.com

Manchester
Tel: 0800 804 6796
Therapist: Rob Groves
Email:
info@easywaymanchester.co.uk
Website: www.allencarr.com

Milton Keynes
Tel: 0800 0197 017
Therapists: Kim Bennett, Emma Hudson
Email: kim@easywaybucks.co.uk
Website: www.allencarr.com

Newcastle/North East
Tel: 0800 077 6187
Therapist: Mark Keen
Email:
info@easywaynortheast.co.uk
Website: www.allencarr.com

Northampton
Tel: 0800 0197 017
Therapists: Kim Bennett, Emma Hudson
Email: kim@easywaybucks.co.uk
Website: www.allencarr.com

Nottingham
Tel: +44 (0)1270 664176
Therapist: Debbie Brewer-West
Email:
debbie@easyway2stopsmoking.co.uk
Website: www.allencarr.com

Oxford
Tel: 0800 0197 017
Therapists: Kim Bennett, Emma Hudson
Email: kim@easywaybucks.co.uk
Website: www.allencarr.com

Peterborough
Freephone: 0800 0197 017
Therapists: Kim Bennett, Emma Hudson
Email: kim@easywaybucks.co.uk
Website: www.allencarr.com

Reading
Tel: 0800 028 7257
Therapists: John Dicey, Colleen Dwyer, Emma Hudson
Email: info@allencarr.com
Website: www.allencarr.com

SCOTLAND
Glasgow and Edinburgh
Tel: +44 (0)131 449 7858
Therapists: Paul Melvin and Jim McCreadie
Email: info@easywayscotland.co.uk
Website: www.allencarr.com

Sheffield
Tel: 0800 804 6796
Therapist: Rob Groves
Email: info@easywayyorkshire.co.uk
Website: www.allencarr.com

Shrewsbury
Tel: +44 (0)1270 664176
Therapist: Debbie Brewer-West
Email: debbie@easyway2stopsmoking.co.uk
Website: www.allencarr.com

Southampton
Tel: 0800 028 7257
Therapists: John Dicey, Colleen Dwyer, Emma Hudson
Email: info@allencarr.com
Website: www.allencarr.com

Southport
Tel: 0800 077 6187
Therapist: Mark Keen
Email: mark@easywaylancashire.co.uk
Website: www.allencarr.com

Staines/Heathrow
Tel: 0800 028 7257
Therapists: John Dicey, Colleen Dwyer, Emma Hudson
Email: info@allencarr.com
Website: www.allencarr.com

Surrey
Park House, 14 Pepys Road, Raynes Park, London SW20 8NH
Tel: +44 (0)20 8944 7761
Fax: +44 (0)20 8944 8619
Therapists: John Dicey, Colleen Dwyer, Crispin Hay, Emma Hudson, Rob Fielding
Email: mail@allencarr.com
Website: www.allencarr.com

Stevenage
Tel: 0800 0197 017
Therapists: Kim Bennett, Emma Hudson
Email: kim@easywaybucks.co.uk
Website: www.allencarr.com

Stoke
Tel: +44 (0)1270 664176
Therapist: Debbie Brewer-West
Email: debbie@easyway2stopsmoking.co.uk
Website: www.allencarr.com

Swindon
Tel: +44 (0)117 950 1441
Therapist: Charles Holdsworth Hunt
Email: stopsmoking@easywaybristol.co.uk
Website: www.allencarr.com

Telford
Tel: +44 (0)1270 664176
Therapist: Debbie Brewer-West
Email: debbie@easyway2stopsmoking.co.uk
Website: www.allencarr.com

WORLDWIDE CLINICS

REPUBLIC OF IRELAND
Dublin and Cork
Lo-Call (From ROI) 1 890 ESYWAY (37 99 29)
Tel: +353 (0)1 499 9010 (4 lines)
Therapists: Brenda Sweeney and Team
Email: info@allencarr.ie
Website: www.allencarr.com

ARGENTINA
Buenos Aires – opening 2012
Website: www.allencarr.com

AUSTRALIA
North Queensland
Tel: 1300 85 11 75
Therapist: Tara Pickard-Clark
Email: nqld@allencarr.com.au
Website: www.allencarr.com

Northern Territory – Darwin
Tel: 1300 55 78 01
Therapist: Dianne Fisher
Email: wa@allencarr.com.au
Website: www.allencarr.com

Sydney, New South Wales
Tel & Fax: 1300 78 51 80
Therapist: Natalie Clays
Email: nsw@allencarr.com.au
Website: www.allencarr.com

South Australia
Tel: 1300 55 78 01
Therapist: Dianne Fisher
Email: wa@allencarr.com.au
Website: www.allencarr.com

South Queensland
Tel: 1300 85 58 06
Therapist: Tara Pickard-Clark
Email: sqld@allencarr.com.au
Website: www.allencarr.com

Victoria, Tasmania, A.C.T.
Tel: +61 (0)3 9894 8866
or 1300 790 565
Therapist: Gail Morris
Email: info@allencarr.com.au
Website: www.allencarr.com

Western Australia
Tel: 1300 55 78 01
Therapist: Dianne Fisher
Email: wa@allencarr.com.au
Website: www.allencarr.com

AUSTRIA
Sessions held throughout Austria
Freephone: 0800RAUCHEN (0800 7202430)
Tel: +43 (0)3512 44755
Therapists: Erich Kellermann and Team
Email: info@allen-carr.at
Website: www.allencarr.com

BELGIUM
Antwerp
Tel: +32 (0)3 281 6255
Fax: +32 (0)3 744 0000
Therapist: Dirk Nielandt
Email: easyway@dirknielandt.be
Website: www.allencarr.com

BRAZIL
São Paulo
Therapists: Alberto Steinberg (tel: (55) (11) 99325-6514), Lilian Brunstein ((55) (11) 99456-0153)
Email: contato@easywaysp.com.br
Website: www.allencarr.com

BULGARIA
Tel: 0800 14104 / +359 899 88 99 07
Therapist: Rumyana Kostadinova
Email: rk@nepushaveche.com
Website: www.allencarr.com

CANADA
Toll free: +1 866 666 4299 / +1 905 849 7736
English Therapist: Damian O'Hara
French Therapist: Rejean Belanger
Regular seminars held in Toronto, Vancouver and Montreal
Corporate programs available throughout Canada
Email: info@theeasywaytostopsmoking.com
Website: www.allencarr.com

CHILE
Tel: +56 2 4744587
Therapist: Claudia Sarmiento
Email: contacto@allencarr.cl
Website: www.allencarr.com

COLOMBIA
Therapist: Felipe Sanint Echeverri
Tel: +57 3158681043
Email: felipesanint@allencarrcolombia.com
www.allencarr.com

CYPRUS
Tel: +357 77 77 78 30
Therapist: Kyriacos Michaelides
Email: info@allencarr.com.cy
Website: www.allencarr.com

DENMARK
Sessions held throughout Denmark
Tel: +45 70267711
Therapist: Mette Fonss
Email: mette@easyway.dk
Website: www.allencarr.com

ECUADOR
Tel & Fax: +593 (0)2 2820 920
Therapist: Ingrid Wittich
Email: toisan@pi.pro.ec
Website: www.allencarr.com

ESTONIA
Tel: +372 733 0044
Therapist: Henry Jakobson
Email: info@allencarr.ee
Website: www.allencarr.com

FINLAND
Tel: +358-(0)45 3544099
Therapist: Janne Ström
Email: info@allencarr.fi
Website: www.allencarr.com

FRANCE
Sessions held throughout France
Freephone: 0800 FUMEUR
Tel: +33 (4) 91 33 54 55
Therapists: Erick Serre and Team
Email: info@allencarr.fr
Website: www.allencarr.com

GERMANY
Sessions held throughout Germany
Freephone: 08000RAUCHEN (0800 07282436)
Tel: +49 (0) 8031 90190-0
Therapists: Erich Kellermann and Team
Email: info@allen-carr.de
Website: www.allencarr.com

GREECE
Sessions held throughout Greece
Tel: +30 210 5224087
Therapist: Panos Tzouras
Email: panos@allencarr.gr
Website: www.allencarr.com

HUNGARY
Budapest
Tel: +36 06 80 624 426
Therapist: Gabor Szasz
Email: szasz.gabor@allencarr.hu
Website: www.allencarr.com

ICELAND
Reykjavik
Tel: +354 588 7060
Therapist: Petur Einarsson
Email: easyway@easyway.is
Website: www.allencarr.com

INDIA
Bangalore & Chennai
Tel: +91 (0)80 41603838
Therapist: Suresh Shottam
Email:
info@easywaytostopsmoking.co.in
Website: www.allencarr.com

ISRAEL
Sessions held throughout Israel
Tel: +972 (0)3 6212525
Therapists: Ramy Romanovsky, Orit Rozen, Kinneret Triffon
Email: info@allencarr.co.il
Website: www.allencarr.com

ITALY
Sessions held throughout Italy
Tel/Fax: +39 (0)2 7060 2438
Therapists: Francesca Cesati and Team
Email: info@easywayitalia.com
Website: www.allencarr.com

JAPAN
Sessions held throughout Japan
www.allencarr.com

LATVIA
Tel: +371 67 27 22 25
Therapists: Anatolijs Ivanovs
Email: info@allencarr.lv
Website: www.allencarr.com

LITHUANIA
Tel: +370 694 29591
Therapist: Evaldas Zvirblis
Email: info@mestirukyti.eu
Website: www.allencarr.com

MAURITIUS
Tel: +230 727 5103
Therapist: Heidi Hoareau
Email: info@allencarr.mu
Website: www.allencarr.com

MEXICO
Sessions held throughout Mexico
Tel: +52 55 2623 0631
Therapists: Jorge Davo and Mario Campuzano Otero
Email: info@allencarr-mexico.com
Website: www.allencarr.com

NETHERLANDS
Sessions held throughout the Netherlands
Allen Carr's Easyway 'stoppen met roken'
Tel: (+31)53 478 43 62 /(+31)900 786 77 37
Email: info@allencarr.nl
Website: www.allencarr.com

NEW ZEALAND
North Island – Auckland
Tel: +64 (0)9 817 5396
Therapist: Vickie Macrae
Email: vickie@easywaynz.co.nz
Website: www.allencarr.com

South Island – Christchurch
Tel: +64 (0)3 326 5464
Therapist: Laurence Cooke
Email: laurence@easywaysouthisland.co.nz
Website: www.allencarr.com

NORWAY
Oslo
Tel: +47 93 20 09 11
Therapist: René Adde
Email: post@easyway-norge.no
Website: www.allencarr.com

PERU
Lima
Tel: +511 637 7310
Therapist: Luis Loranca
Email:
lloranca@dejardefumaraltoque.com
Website: www.allencarr.com

POLAND
Sessions held throughout Poland
Tel: +48 (0)22 621 36 11
Therapist: Anna Kabat
Email: info@allen-carr.pl
Website: www.allencarr.com

PORTUGAL
Oporto
Tel: +351 22 9958698
Therapist: Ria Slof
Email:
info@comodeixardefumar.com
Website: www.allencarr.com

ROMANIA
Tel: +40 (0) 7321 3 8383
Therapist: Diana Vasiliu
Email: raspunsuri@allencarr.ro
Website: www.allencarr.com

RUSSIA
Moscow
Tel: +7 495 644 64 26
Therapist: Fomin Alexander
Email: info@allencarr.ru
Website: www.allencarr.com
St Petersburg – opening 2012
Website: www.allencarr.com

SERBIA
Belgrade
Tel: +381 (0)11 308 8686
Email: office@allencarr.co.rs / milos.rakovic@allencarr.co.rs
Website: www.allencarr.com

SINGAPORE
Tel: +65 6329 9660
Therapist: Pam Oei
Email: pam@allencarr.com.sg
Website: www.allencarr.com

SLOVENIA
– opening 2012
Website: www.allencarr.com

SOUTH AFRICA
Sessions held throughout South Africa
National Booking Line: 0861 100 200
Head Office
15 Draper Square, Draper St, Claremont 7708, Cape Town
Cape Town: Dr Charles Nel
Tel: +27 (0)21 851 5883
Mobile: 083 600 5555
Therapists: Dr Charles Nel, Dudley Garner, Malcolm Robinson and Team
Email: easyway@allencarr.co.za
Website: www.allencarr.com

SPAIN
Madrid – Opening 2012

Marbella
Tel: +44 8456 187306
Therapist: Charles Holdsworth Hunt
Email: stopsmoking@easywaymarbella.com
Sessions held in English
Website: www.allencarr.com

SWEDEN
Göteborg
Tel: +46 (0)8 240100
Email: info@allencarr.nu
Website: www.allencarr.com

Malmö
Tel: +46 (0) 40 30 24 00
Email: info@allencarr.nu
Website: www.allencarr.com

Stockholm
Tel: +46 (0) 735 000 123
Therapist: Christofer Elde
Email: kontakt@allencarr.se
Website: www.allencarr.com

SWITZERLAND
Sessions held throughout Switzerland
Freephone: 0800RAUCHEN (0800/728 2436)
Tel: +41 (0)52 383 3773
Fax: +41 (0)52 383 3774
Therapists: Cyrill Argast and Team
For sessions in Suisse Romand and Svizzera Italiana:
Tel: 0800 386 387
Email: info@allen-carr.ch
Website: www.allencarr.com

TURKEY
Sessions held throughout Turkey
Tel: +90 212 358 5307
Therapist: Emre Ustunucar
Email: info@allencarrturkiye.com
Website: www.allencarr.com

UKRAINE
Crimea, Simferopol
Tel: +38 095 781 8180
Therapist: Yuri Zhvakolyuk
Email: zhvakolyuk@gmail.com
Website: www.allencarr.com

Kiev
Tel: +38 044 353 2934
Therapist: Kirill Stekhin
Email: kirill@allencarr.kiev.ua
Website: www.allencarr.com

USA

Central information and bookings:
Toll free: 1 866 666 4299 / New York: 212- 330 9194
Email: info@theeasywaytostopsmoking.com
Website: www.allencarr.com
Seminars held regularly in New York, Los Angeles, Denver and Houston
Corporate programs available throughout the USA
Mailing address: 1133 Broadway, Suite 706, New York, NY 10010
Therapists: Damian O'Hara, Collene Curran

OTHER ALLEN CARR BOOKS

Allen Carr's Stop Smoking Now
ISBN: 978-1-84837-373-0

Allen Carr's Illustrated Easy Way for Women to Stop Smoking
ISBN: 978-0-572-03398-9

Allen Carr's Easy Way to Stop Smoking Kit (with 2 x audio CDs)
ISBN: 978-1-84837-498-0

Allen Carr's Illustrated Easy Way to Stop Smoking
ISBN: 978-1-84837-930-5

Allen Carr's How to Be a Happy Non-Smoker
ISBN: 978-0-572-03163-3

Allen Carr's Smoking Sucks (Parent Guide with 16 page pull-out comic)
ISBN: 978-0-572-03320-0

Allen Carr's No More Ashtrays
ISBN: 978-1-84858-083-1

Allen Carr's Easy Way to Control Alcohol
ISBN: 978-1-84837-465-2

Allen Carr's No More Hangovers
ISBN: 978-1-84837-555-0

Allen Carr's Lose Weight Now
ISBN: 978-1-84837-720-2

Allen Carr's No More Diets
ISBN: 978-1-84837-554-3

Allen Carr's No More Worrying
ISBN: 978-1-84837-826-1

Available from all good book retailers

DISCOUNT VOUCHER
for
ALLEN CARR'S
EASYWAY CLINICS

Recover the price of this book when you attend an
Allen Carr's Easyway Clinic
anywhere in the world!

Allen Carr's Easyway has a global network of stop smoking clinics where we guarantee you'll find it easy to stop smoking or your money back.

The success rate based on this unique money-back guarantee is over 90%.

Sessions addressing weight, alcohol and other drug addictions are also available at certain clinics.

When you book your session, mention this voucher and you'll receive a discount to the value of this book. Contact your nearest clinic for more information on how the sessions work and to book your appointment.

Details of Allen Carr's Easyway Clinics can be found at

www.allencarr.com
or call 0800 389 2115

This offer is not valid in conjunction with any other offer/promotion.